Goose berry Patch Co. ™

A Country Store In Your Mailbox℠

Celebrate Autumn

...crisp, apple-red days and cozy nights

DEBORAH S. SORKIN
3305 FOX RUN COURT
MORGANTOWN, WV 26505
(304) 594-2711

A Country Store In Your Mailbox℠

Gooseberry Patch
P.O. Box 190, Dept. CELA
Delaware, OH 43015

1·800·85·GOOSE
1·800·854·6673

Copyright 1996, Gooseberry Patch
1-888052-02-3
First Printing 30,000 copies, June, 1996

How To Subscribe

Would you like to receive
"A Country Store in Your Mailbox"℠?
For a 2-year subscription to our
Gooseberry Patch catalog
simply send $3.00 to:
Gooseberry Patch
P.O. Box 190, Dept. CELA
Delaware, OH 43015

Printed in the United States of America
TOOF COOKBOOK DIVISION

STARR ★ TOOF

670 South Cooper Street
Memphis, TN 38104

Contents

Dedication

To all of our friends who find
happiness in golden harvest moons,
freshly-picked apples,
scarlet leaves dancing in the wind,
scary pumpkins & family gathered 'round the table.

Appreciation

Thanks to our Gooseberry Family
for giving us new reasons
to celebrate every season.

Farmhouse Breakfast

...hearty morning fare for that chill in the air

Country Ham and Cheese Omelet
Zucchini Frittata with Squash Blossoms
Oven-Baked French Toast
Fresh Berry Butter
American Home Fries
Overnight Buckwheat Cakes
Breakfast Butternut Squash
Gravy-Lover's Buttermilk Biscuits

There were three ravens sat on a tree,
They were as black as they might be.
The one of them said to his mate,
'Where shall we our breakfast take?'
- Anonymous

Raspberry Jam

Farmhouse Breakfast

Country Ham and Cheese Omelet

Nothing beats the taste of farm-fresh eggs for breakfast.

1 cooked potato, thinly sliced
1/2 onion, thinly sliced
5 T. butter
salt and pepper to taste
1/2 c. cooked ham, diced

4 eggs, beaten with 1 t.
   water
1/2 c. cheddar cheese,
   shredded
parsley

Sauté potato and onion in 2 tablespoons melted butter until cooked and tender. Add salt and pepper. Stir in ham and cook until crisp. In a separate omelet pan or skillet, melt 2 tablespoons butter. When butter bubbles, pour in well-beaten eggs. Over low heat, as eggs begin to thicken, add ham, onion and potato across the center. With wide spatula, gently lift egg mixture from bottom of pan around all sides until nearly cooked, but still slightly runny on top. Sprinkle cheese on top of omelet. Lift one half of omelet mixture and fold over on top of the other half. Slide out of pan onto warmed plate. Garnish with parsley. Serves 2.

I like the fall, the mist and all.
I like the night owl's lonely call —
And wailing sound of wind around.
I like the gray November day,
And bare, dead boughs that coldly sway
Against my pane. I like the rain.
I like to sit and laugh at it —
And tend my cozy fire a bit.
I like the fall — the mist and all.

- Dixie Willson

Zucchini Frittata with Squash Blossoms

The squash blossoms are delicious and add color and texture.

6 eggs, beaten
1/4 c. Parmesan cheese, finely
   grated
1 T. fresh parsley, coarsely
   chopped
1 garlic clove, minced

salt and pepper to taste
2 T. butter
1 lb. small green zucchini,
   thinly sliced
12 squash blossoms, cut into
   strips

Preheat the broiler. In a deep bowl, beat the eggs, cheese, parsley, garlic, salt and pepper. Heat 1 tablespoon butter in a large iron skillet. Add the zucchini and cook until tender, about 10 minutes. Add the squash blossoms during the last 5 minutes. Remove vegetables from heat and add to egg mixture. Heat remaining butter in skillet. When the pan is hot, reduce heat to medium and add egg mixture. Cook until nearly set, about 8 minutes. Put the pan under the broiler for about 30 seconds, or until top is lightly browned. Slide the frittata onto a serving plate. Serves 3 or 4.

Buttery soft, ripe avocado tastes delicious with eggs and cheese, and is filled with vitamins. Scoop balls of soft avocado with a melon ball cutter and pile into a pretty bowl. Top with a sprinkle of lemon juice to prevent discoloration. Bits of crisp bacon make a nice garnish.

Farmhouse Breakfast

Oven-Baked French Toast

Warm cinnamon taste on a frosty fall morning!

1/3 c. butter
6 large eggs
1 1/2 c. milk
1 1/2 T. confectioner's sugar

1 t. vanilla
1/2 t. cinnamon
12 slices thick white bread

Heat oven to 425 degrees. Have one oven rack in lowest position and the other in the middle. Grease two cookie sheets with 1 tablespoon butter each. Lightly beat eggs; stir in milk, confectioner's sugar, vanilla, and cinnamon. Dip bread in egg mixture; coat both sides. Place 6 slices coated bread on each sheet. Dot with butter. Place a sheet on each rack. Bake 15 minutes, switching pans once, until bread is golden brown. Dust with confectioner's sugar or top with Fresh Berry Butter or strawberry jam.

Have you ever gone into a farmhouse kitchen on a baking day, and seen the great crock of dough set by the fire to rise? If you have, and if you were at that time still young enough to be interested in everything you saw, you will remember that you found yourself quite unable to resist the temptation to poke your finger into the soft round dough that curved inside the pan like a giant mushroom. And you will remember that your finger made a dent in the dough, and that slowly, but quite surely, the dent disappeared, and the dough looked quite the same as it did before you touched it. Unless, of course, your hand was extra dirty in which case, naturally, there would be a little black mark.

- E. Nesbit

American Home Fries

1/4 lb. bacon
2 lbs. gold or white potatoes, peeled and sliced 1/8" thick

2 onions, peeled and coarsely chopped
salt and pepper to taste

You will need two nonstick 10-inch skillets. Divide the bacon between the two skillets and fry until crisp. Remove with a slotted spoon and set aside. Wash the potato slices and pat them dry. In the hot bacon fat, stir-fry half of the potatoes in each skillet for about 3 minutes. Add the onions and season with salt and pepper. Partially cover the skillets and cook home fries over medium-low heat for 15 minutes, stirring occasionally. Top with crumbled bacon and serve immediately. Serves 4.

If you wash the sliced potatoes before frying, this will remove the surface starch, resulting in a crisper home fry.

 ## Fresh Berry Butter

Make plenty to go 'round for pancakes, French toast, waffles and English muffins.

1 pint fresh, clean raspberries, strawberries or blackberries

1 c. butter, softened to room temperature
2 c. confectioner's sugar

Combine berries, butter and sugar and beat until soft and lumpy.

Keep fresh berries from bruising by storing them on a baking sheet in a single layer in your refrigerator. Keeping them apart will also help prevent mold. To freeze fresh berries, place in a single layer in your freezer. Once frozen, transfer to freezer bags.

Overnight Buckwheat Cakes

Tender and fluffy, with hearty flavor.

1/4 yeast cake
3/4 c. lukewarm water
1/2 t. salt
1 3/4 c. buckwheat flour

1 1/2 c. scalded milk
1 t. baking soda
1 T. molasses
1 egg, beaten

Soften yeast in 1/4 cup water. Stir salt, yeast and flour into lukewarm scalded milk. Beat well; cover and let stand in a warm place overnight. In the morning, dissolve soda in 1/2 cup warm water and add to flour mixture. Add molasses and egg. Bake on hot griddle, turning cakes only once. Makes 6-8 medium-sized cakes.

Pamper your coffee lovers with fresh cream, raw cane sugar, and shakers of cinnamon and cocoa. Offer whipped cream for a special treat! Tea lovers will appreciate selecting from herbal, black or green varieties, along with fresh lemon and honey.

Breakfast Butternut Squash

A healthful side dish that goes well with omelets or hotcakes.

1 lb. butternut squash,
   peeled, seeded and sliced
2 T. vegetable oil
1 clove garlic, minced
1/2 t. ginger root, grated
1 c. broccoli flowerets

1/2 c. celery, sliced
1 t. fresh onion, finely
   chopped
1 T. lemon juice
2 t. honey

Stir-fry the sliced squash (1/4-inch slices) in the vegetable oil over medium-high heat, along with the garlic, and ginger root for about 3 minutes. Add broccoli, celery and onion and sauté 3 to 4 minutes longer, until vegetables are crisp-tender. Combine lemon juice with honey and toss into vegetables. You may top with sunflower seeds or raisins if desired.

Fill a large basket with bright oranges for a beautiful breakfast centerpiece.

Gravy-Lover's Buttermilk Biscuits

If you're serving sausage, this is the biscuit to bake.

1 1/2 c. flour
1 T. baking powder
1/4 t. baking soda
1 T. sugar

1/2 t. salt
1/2 c. butter
1/4 c. buttermilk
1 T. heavy cream

Preheat oven to 400 degrees. Grease a large baking sheet. Sift dry ingredients into a large bowl. Cut in butter until mixture resembles rolled oats. Cover and refrigerate 20 minutes. Make a well in the center of the mixture and add enough buttermilk to hold it together. Stir quickly with your fingers until just combined. Turn mixture onto a lightly floured board and roll into a 3/4-inch thick square. Cut as many biscuits as you can with a biscuit cutter and place on greased baking sheet, about 1 inch apart. Brush the tops of the biscuits with the cream. Bake 13-15 minutes, until golden. Serve with berry butter, fresh sweet butter, honey, or sausage gravy.

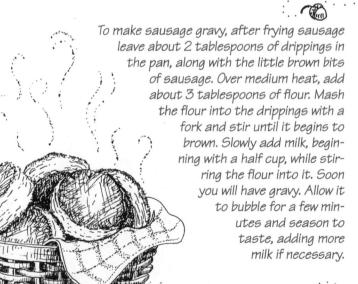

To make sausage gravy, after frying sausage leave about 2 tablespoons of drippings in the pan, along with the little brown bits of sausage. Over medium heat, add about 3 tablespoons of flour. Mash the flour into the drippings with a fork and stir until it begins to brown. Slowly add milk, beginning with a half cup, while stirring the flour into it. Soon you will have gravy. Allow it to bubble for a few minutes and season to taste, adding more milk if necessary.

Inspirations...

Zucchini Ribbons

Dress up your omelet or frittata platter with thin ribbons of zucchini. They're easy to make...just use a sharp vegetable peeler to cut the zucchini lengthwise into long, thin strips from end to end. Pour boiling water over the strips to cover, let stand for a minute, then drain and follow with cool water. Wind the ribbons around the ends of your serving platter, or arrange on individual serving plates.

Flavored Butters

Create a variety of flavored butters for your breakfast table. Delicious on pancakes, breads, muffins or in a bowl of oatmeal! Simply soften a stick of butter and mix it with flavorings of your choice. Then spoon butter mixture across a sheet of waxed paper, roll into a log, wrap tightly and refrigerate. Try these combinations: a teaspoon of grated orange peel and some dried mint leaves for tangy orange-mint butter; grated lemon peel and poppy seeds for lemon-poppy seed butter; 1/2 cup ground hazelnuts and ground cinnamon for cinnamon-nut butter. Experiment with different mixtures of citrus, nuts and spices. Your butter will store in the freezer up to two months.

Sunrise Orange Juice

Make orange juice really special. Freeze cranberry juice cocktail into ice cubes, then fill your juice pitcher and glasses with cranberry cubes before adding freshly-squeezed orange juice.

Corn-Tomato Sunflowers

Dress up a platter of sausages or eggs with these pretty garnishes. Blanch a husked ear of corn in boiling water for a minute, then drain and run cold water over it until cool. Holding the corn with one hand, cut it into 1/4-inch slices with a very sharp or serrated knife. These will be the petals of your "sunflower." Slice cherry tomatoes in half. Place the tomatoes, cut side down, in the centers of each slice of corn.

Indian Summer Picnic

...the glory of October spread out before you

Fresh Veggie Pizza
Spicy Black Bean Salsa
Crunchy Baked Pita Chips
Picnic Barbecued Chicken Sandwiches
Favorite Peanut Butter Cookies
Spiced Apple Cider

*There is something in the autumn
that is native to my blood —
Touch of manner, hint of mood,
And my heart is like a rhyme,
With the yellow and the purple
and the crimson keeping time.*

- Bliss Carman

Fresh Veggie Pizza

This crunchy portable snack recipe can be adapted to your favorite vegetables. Try experimenting with additional ingredients like olives, mushrooms and green peppers.

2 pkg. refrigerated
   crescent rolls
2-8 oz. pkg. of
   cream cheese, softened
1 c. mayonnaise
1 pkg. dry ranch salad
   dressing mix

1/4 c. green onion, sliced
1/2 c. carrots, shredded
1/4 c. cauliflower pieces
1/4 c. broccoli pieces
1/2 c. tomatoes, chopped
3/4 c. cheddar cheese,
   shredded

Press crescent roll dough onto pizza pan. Bake at 350 degrees for 10 minutes. Mix cream cheese, mayonnaise, and dressing mix. Spread on baked crust. Top with vegetables. Press into cream cheese mixture. Sprinkle with cheddar cheese. Refrigerate, covered, for 2 hours. Serves 8.

The best of all sauces is exercise in the open air and, equally, the best of digestives is pleasant company.

-St. Ange

Spicy Black Bean Salsa

A quick and easy low-fat salsa, hot as you like!

8 oz. can black beans,
   drained and rinsed
2/3 c. corn relish
1/4 c. onion, minced

2 t. lime juice
1/4 t. ground cumin
hot pepper sauce to taste

Stir all ingredients together and allow to stand, covered for 30 minutes. Serve with baked pita chips.

Crunchy Baked Pita Chips

Chewier and fresher-tasting than bagged chips.

4 large rounds of pita bread
1 t. garlic powder

Split pita bread rounds, then cut into wedges. Sprinkle with garlic powder and bake in a single layer in a 350 degree oven for 10 to 12 minutes, or until crisp. Store in an airtight container.

You may find a listing of bike paths in your area at the local library. There are few better ways to enjoy the fall colors than a tree-lined bike path, under canopies of red, russet and gold.

Picnic Barbecued Chicken Sandwiches

These are delicious hot or cold, depending on where you'll be enjoying them.

3 lbs. chicken thighs and
    breasts, skinned, cooked,
    boned and shredded
1 c. catsup
1 3/4 c. water
1 onion, finely chopped
1 t. salt

1 t. celery seed
1 t. chili powder
1/4 c. brown sugar, packed
1 t. hot pepper sauce
1/4 c. Worcestershire sauce
1/4 c. red wine vinegar
6 Kaiser rolls

Combine all ingredients except rolls in large saucepan and simmer for 1 1/2 hours. Pile onto Kaiser rolls. Pack in a thermal container with ice and serve cold.

Keep chicken sandwiches and other cold things cold by packing a few frozen juice boxes in with your picnic treats.

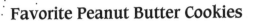

Favorite Peanut Butter Cookies

For extra crunch, you may add whole peanuts to the batter.

1/2 c. unsalted butter,
   softened
1/2 c. sugar
1/2 c. brown sugar, firmly
   packed
1 large egg

1 c. smooth or chunky
   peanut butter
1/2 t. baking soda
1/2 t. vanilla
1 1/4 c. all-purpose flour

Preheat oven to 350 degrees. Cream butter and sugars until light and fluffy. Add egg, peanut butter, soda, and vanilla and beat until smooth. Add flour in portions, beating until well mixed. Shape balls out of teaspoonfuls of the dough and arrange on greased baking sheets. Flatten balls with tines of a fork, making a pattern. Bake in center of oven about 12 minutes, or until golden. Makes 70 2-inch cookies.

Spiced Apple Cider

Is there anything that tastes more like autumn than cider?

3 qts. apple cider
12 whole cloves
10 whole allspice
1 T. candied ginger
10 cinnamon sticks
3/4 c. brown sugar,
   packed

Combine all ingredients except sugar and boil. Lower heat, add sugar and simmer 15-20 minutes. Strain and pack in thermos container to serve steaming hot.

Indian Summer Picnic

Great ideas...

Applesauce Leather

Kids love this delicious, portable snack with just three ingredients. Just take a 16-ounce jar of applesauce and season with 1/4 teaspoon ground cinnamon and 1/2 teaspoon fresh lemon juice. Puree the mixture until smooth. Spread it on a large piece of plastic wrap so that it measures about 1/4-inch thick. Let it dry in the oven, with the door slightly ajar, at 150 degrees about 6-8 hours, or until it feels somewhat dry but still tacky. Remove it from the plastic wrap, rolling it into a jellyroll shape. Then cut it into smaller portions. Store covered in your refrigerator, or in a cooler.

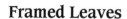

Framed Leaves

Everyone agrees, autumn leaves are a work of art. Why not frame them? Make a simple mounting board with a piece of cork from a building supply store; just have the cork cut to fit inside a wooden frame. Old worn frames look best...they have that antique look we love. You can cover the cork with fabric to complement your colors. Just stretch the fabric over the cork and staple to the back. Arrange leaves and glue to the fabric. Then fit the cork inside the frame and use a tackhammer to pound tacks or fine nails through the cork and the back of the frame. Attach a fine wire or sawtoothed brad to the back for hanging.

Decorated Pots

There are so many ways to decorate terra cotta pots! Gather colorful leaves, pine cones, acorns, seed pods, dried berries and cattails and arrange into a pleasing pattern. Then hot-glue your treasures to flowerpots. Use a large pot with a candle as a centerpiece, or fill smaller pots with potpourri.

Golden Wheat Bundles

Gather stalks of wheat and combine with dried flowers to make a beautiful wall hanging. Take three lengths of raffia (about 3 ft. each) and braid together. Then form a bunch of dried wheat and flowers (everlastings work well) and gradually layer the heads down the sides to form a pleasing shape. Tie the bunch with twine in three places, spaced equally apart. Add another layer of wheat and flowers, tying in their stems about 2/3 of the way down. Fan out all the stems at the base, then trim them squarely at the bottom. Wrap fine wire around the center for hanging. Tie your raffia braid in a bow around the bundle, hiding the wire.

Indian Summer Picnic

TREES

Trees are the kindest things I know,
they do no harm, they simply grow.
And spread a shade for sleepy cows,
and gather birds among their boughs.
They give us fruit in leaves above,
and wood to make our houses of,
and leaves to burn on Halloween,
and in the spring new buds of green.
They are the first when day's begun
to touch the beams of morning sun,
they are the last to hold the light
when evening changes into night.
And when a moon floats on the sky
they hum a drowsy lullaby
of sleepy children long ago...
Trees are the kindest things I know.

- Harry Behn

Tailgate Gathering
...hearty fare for football frenzy

Soft Pretzels with Mustard
Running Back Popcorn 'n Peanuts
Championship Artichoke Dip
Halftime Tomato-Basil Soup
Salami Submarine with Olive Salad
Confetti Salad
Ohio State Buckeyes
End Zone Brownies

SEPTEMBER
A road like brown ribbon,
A sky that is blue,
A forest of green
With the sky peeping through.
Asters, deep purple,
A grasshopper's call,
Today it is summer,
Tomorrow is fall.
- Edwina Fallis

Soft Pretzels with Mustard

You may want to triple this recipe...warm, chewy pretzels are very popular!

2 pkg. dry yeast
1 1/2 c. warm water
4 1/2 c. flour

1/2 t. salt
1/4 c. baking soda in 1 c. water
yellow, Dijon, and spicy brown
   mustards

Dissolve yeast in warm water. Sift flour into large bowl. Add yeast and salt to flour. Mix well and allow to rise about 15 minutes. Roll in long strips about 8 inches long and place in shallow pan in soda solution for 2 minutes. Form into desired shapes and place on greased cookie sheet. Sprinkle with salt as desired. Bake at 350 degrees for 20 minutes. Makes 12 pretzels. Serve with assortment of mustards.

No tickets to the big game? Have a tailgate party anyway! Soak up the atmosphere by going to a local high school pep rally or pre-game party. Wear the team colors and cheer them on.

Running Back Popcorn 'n Peanuts

You'll go "running back" for more!

1/2 c. honey
1/4 c. butter

6 c. popped popcorn
1 c. salted peanuts

Heat honey and butter until blended. Mix popcorn and peanuts in a large bowl, and stir in honey butter mixture. Spread mixture into 2 large pans. Bake for 10 minutes at 350 degrees.

No one knows who discovered popcorn, but it's been around for centuries. In ancient times, it was believed that each popcorn kernel had a little devil inside. When the kernel was heated, the little devil became so angry that he burst through the hull trying to escape. The Aztecs used popcorn as decoration on headdresses, statues, and in good luck ceremonies. It is believed that popcorn was introduced to the English colonists at the first Thanksgiving. The colonists often served popcorn as a breakfast cereal hot or cold with sugar and cream.

Tailgate Gathering

Championship Artichoke Dip

Try serving this hot, cheesy dip in a scooped-out round of sour-dough bread. Just brush the insides with olive oil and bake in a 350 degree oven for 10 minutes.

2 c. Parmesan cheese
2 c. mozzarella cheese
1 c. mayonnaise

2 cloves garlic, finely chopped
16 oz. can artichoke hearts, drained and finely chopped

Mix all ingredients thoroughly. Bake at 380 degrees for 45 minutes. Serve with an assortment of crackers.

Half Time Tomato-Basil Soup

A thermos of this spicy soup will warm you to your toes.

1 large onion, chopped
1/2 c. butter
6 ripe tomatoes, chopped

2/3 c. sherry
6-8 fresh basil leaves
1 c. cheddar cheese, grated

Sauté onion in butter until golden. Add tomatoes, sherry and basil, cover loosely and simmer 30 minutes. Mash large chunks of tomato with a potato masher. Serve with croutons and top with cheese.

Salami Submarine with Olive Salad

A favorite craving of some men we know.

18-inch long loaf of crusty
French bread
1 qt. olive salad (see
below)

1/4 lb. Genoa salami,
thinly sliced
1/4 lb. Swiss cheese,
thinly sliced

Open the bread lengthwise but do not cut all the way through to the other side. Scoop out some of the bread from each half. Divide the olive salad and pack into each half. Layer salami and cheese in rows down each half of the sandwich. Close the halves together and wrap tightly in heavy aluminum foil. To fully blend the flavors, place heavy books on top of the sandwich and allow it to rest for a couple of hours. When ready to serve, slice into 2-inch portions. Serves 9.

Put your foil-wrapped sub in the oven for 20 minutes; then sprinkle Italian dressing under the bun for a hot, crisp treat. For extra tang, add banana peppers, too.

Olive Salad:

3 c. Greek, green, and black
olives, sliced off the pit
7 oz. jar roasted red peppers,
chopped
2 T. capers, drained

1/2 c. fresh parsley, chopped
1/4 c. fresh basil, chopped
2 garlic cloves, crushed
3 T. red wine vinegar
6 T. olive oil

Toss all ingredients together and store in a tightly covered glass jar in the refrigerator. This salad improves with age and is delicious on many sandwiches.

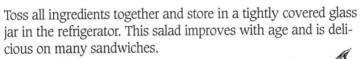

Confetti Salad

You may use bottled dressing, or make your own with a little oil, tarragon or wine vinegar and a touch of sugar.

1 zucchini, shredded
1 carrot, shredded
1 green pepper, shredded

1 yellow squash, shredded
1 sweet red pepper, shredded
1/3 c. vinaigrette or sweet
and sour dressing

Shred all vegetables together and toss with dressing. Serves 4 to 6.

Ohio State Buckeyes

We pay homage to an O.S.U. tradition.

1lb. butter, softened
2 lbs. creamy peanut butter

3 lbs. confectioner's sugar
3 c. dipping chocolate, melted

Cream together butter and peanut butter. Add confectioner's sugar and blend well. Shape mixture by hand into buckeye-sized balls. Place on cookie sheet and refrigerate for one hour. Melt dipping chocolate in top of double boiler. Using a toothpick, dip balls into chocolate 3/4 of the way up. Place on waxed paper and allow to cool. Makes about 200 buckeyes. Can be frozen and kept 2-3 weeks.

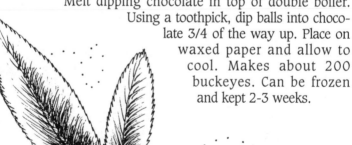

End Zone Brownies

So easy...add chocolate chips for even more rich flavor.

1 stick butter	1 c. plus 1 T. flour
1 c. sugar	1 t. vanilla
4 eggs	1 c. chopped walnuts
16 oz. can chocolate syrup	powdered sugar

Mix all ingredients together and pour into a large greased jelly roll pan. Bake at 350 for 20-22 minutes. Cool 10 minutes, remove from pan and dust with powdered sugar.

Now is the hour that lies between
bright day and night,
When in the dusk the fire blooms
in tongues of light,
And the cat comes to bask herself
in the soft heat,
And Madame Peace draws up her chair
to warm her feet.

- Elizabeth Coatsworth

Break out the fall cookie cutters: autumn leaves, acorns, squirrels...trace around them to make stencils, then dust your brownies over the stencils with powdered sugar for fun fall designs.

Tailgate Gathering

Fun & fancy...

Beer & Soda Buckets

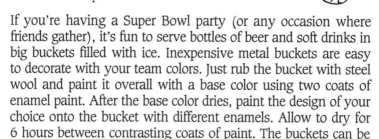

If you're having a Super Bowl party (or any occasion where friends gather), it's fun to serve bottles of beer and soft drinks in big buckets filled with ice. Inexpensive metal buckets are easy to decorate with your team colors. Just rub the bucket with steel wool and paint it overall with a base color using two coats of enamel paint. After the base color dries, paint the design of your choice onto the bucket with different enamels. Allow to dry for 6 hours between contrasting coats of paint. The buckets can be given away as prizes...or save them for the next party!

Colorful Apple Baskets

Those pretty red-handled wooden apple baskets are beautiful filled with bundles of sunny fall grasses and flowers. Try any combination of strawflowers, everlastings, roses, pussy willow, cat tails, yarrow and hydrangeas. Paint your basket freehand, or use stencils to brush on a pretty design. (You can use cookie cutters to make stencils.)

Frightful Fun on All-Hallow's Eve

...spooky ways for kids to celebrate

Goblin Cheese Balls
Midnight Moon Sandwiches
Mummy's Corn Pudding
Frightfully Good Pumpkin Bread
Ghostly Parfaits
Witch's Brew

BLACK AND GOLD
Everything is black and gold,
Black and gold, tonight:
Yellow pumpkins, yellow moon,
Yellow candlelight;
Jet-black cat with golden eyes,
Shadows black as ink,
Firelight blinking in the dark
With a yellow blink.
Black and gold, black and gold,
Nothing in between —
When the world turns
black and gold,
Then it's Halloween!
- Nancy Byrd Turner

Goblin Cheese Balls

Kids and adults alike love this melty cheese appetizer.

1 c. cheddar cheese, shredded
3 T. butter, softened
1/2 c. flour

dash of paprika
dash of salt
1 jar pimento-stuffed
   olives, drained

In a small bowl, blend all ingredients except olives to make a dough. Mold 1 teaspoon dough around each green olive, covering completely. Arrange in ungreased pan and bake in 400 degree oven for 12 minutes. Makes 16 appetizers.

Midnight Moon Sandwiches

*Of course you can vary the sandwich fillings. Try this recipe
with chicken or turkey.*

1 can refrigerated crescent rolls
8 oz. cooked ham, sliced thin
1 c. Monterey Jack cheese, shredded

1 egg, beaten
1/4 stick butter, melted

Open crescent rolls and place on large baking sheet. Layer ham and cheese in the middle of each crescent. Roll into crescents and pinch together edges to seal. Brush tops with egg and melted butter. Bake in 350 degree oven for 15 minutes, or until golden brown. Allow to cool before serving. Makes 8 sandwiches.

Mummy's Corn Pudding

If you have it, try this dish using fresh sweet corn. Yum!

16 oz. can corn, drained
16 oz. can creamed corn
2 eggs, beaten
8 oz. pkg. corn muffin
mix

1/2 c. butter or margarine,
melted
1 c. sour cream
2 c. cheddar cheese, shredded

Mix all ingredients together except cheese. Pour into greased 13"
x 9" baking dish. Bake at 350 degrees for 15 minutes. Sprinkle
with cheese and bake 15 minutes longer. Makes 6 servings.

Frightfully Good Pumpkin Bread

Takes a bit longer to bake than most quick breads...
but well worth it!

3 c. flour
1 1/2 c. sugar
1 1/2 t. cinnamon
1 t. soda
1 t. salt
3/4 t. nutmeg
3/4 t. cloves, ground

1/2 t. baking powder
3 eggs
1 c. vegetable oil
16 oz. can pumpkin
1 c. golden seedless raisins
1/2 c. walnuts, chopped

Preheat oven to 350. Grease and flour two 8 1/2" x 4 1/2" loaf
pans. Combine flour, sugar, cinnamon, soda, salt, nutmeg,
cloves and baking powder in large bowl and mix. In medium
bowl, beat eggs, oil and pumpkin until blended. Stir pumpkin
mixture into flour mixture until flour is moistened. Stir in raisins
and walnuts. Pour into loaf pans and bake for 75 minutes, or
until inserted toothpick comes out clean. Cool in pans 10 minutes, then turn onto wire rack to cool completely.

Mini pumpkins and gourds look festive in a fall
centerpiece or tied onto grapevine wreaths.

Ghostly Parfaits

A fun treat for kids.

2 pkg. (4-serving size) chocolate-flavored instant pudding
3 1/2 c. cold milk
12 oz. container whipped topping

1 pkg. chocolate sandwich cookies, crushed
15-8 oz. clear plastic cups
candy corn and chocolate mini-chips

Make pudding as directed on package, using milk. Stir in 3 cups of the whipped topping and 1/2 of the crushed cookies. Layer pudding and remaining crushed cookies in cups. Top with large, ghost-shaped dollops of whipped topping. Make eyes, nose and mouth with mini-chips, and decorate with candy corn.

This year, invent new designs for your jack-o-lanterns by using Halloween cookie cutters. Trace around the cutters with a marker, then cut out your shapes. Try stacking three different sizes of pumpkins on top of one another to make a pumpkin totem.

Witch's Brew

Serve it up in a cauldron for spooky parties!

1/2 c. cinnamon candies
1/2 c. lemon juice concentrate
1 qt. apple juice

3 T. brown sugar
6 whole cloves
2 red apples, cored
and sliced into rings

In heavy saucepan, melt candies in lemon juice over low heat, stirring frequently. Add apple juice, brown sugar and cloves. Simmer for 15 minutes. Remove cloves and pour into punch bowl or cauldron. Garnish with apple rings. Can be served hot or iced.

Clever tricks & little treats...

Jack-o-Lantern Lollipop Treat

Decorate your jack-o-lantern; then outline a place for his hair. Drill lots of small holes into the pumpkin's head where the hair would be. Then stick colorful lollipops into the holes. Your pumpkin suddenly has a scary hairdo! A fun treat for an elementary school Halloween party. Let the kids pick a lollipop treat from the pumpkin's head.

Popcorn Wreath

Greet goblins and visitors alike with this fun popcorn wreath for your door. Pop two unsalted bags of microwave popcorn (or three if you want to munch!) and pour onto a cookie sheet. Cover a small section of a straw wreath with hot glue and press the popcorn into it. Repeat gluing and pressing the popcorn into the wreath until the entire wreath is covered. Tie a big raffia or orange and black bow to the top of the wreath, and attach a whimsical cut-out (a wicked witch, pumpkin or black cat) to dangle from the center ribbons. After Halloween, remove the ribbons and hang your wreath on a tree limb...welcome treats for squirrels and sparrows!

Pumpkin Cookie Pops

Bake pumpkin-shaped cookies and insert wooden pop sticks into the cookies before baking. Decorate, then wrap each cookie pop with plastic wrap and finish with orange curly ribbon.

Haunted House Hunt

A spooky older kids' party game: Put objects around a room that are scary to the touch. Use torn cotton balls for spiders' webs, olives in a glass of water for eyeballs, an oak leaf for a bat's wing, a pickle for a witch's nose and chicken bones for a skeleton. Let one person at a time wear a blindfold and lead him around to explore the haunted room, telling him what he's touching: this is the spider's nest; this is the witch's nose, etc. See if he can guess what the objects really are; have a special Halloween treat as the prize. Don't forget to play spooky music!

Roasted Pumpkin Seeds

Save fresh pumpkin seeds from your jack-o-lantern. Coat them in a little vegetable oil and a sprinkling of salt, then bake in a 350 degree oven for about 10 minutes. You can make a sweet variation of this crunchy treat by coating the seeds in butter, brown sugar and cinnamon.

 Some romantic Halloween folklore...

If you are born on Halloween, you can tell the future in dreams.

If you drop two needles into a bowl of water, you can tell by the way they move in the water whether you and your true love will meet.

On Halloween, you can scratch some names into several apples and put them into a tub of water. Then bob for the apples. The one you catch will bear the name of your future husband.

If you walk into a room backward at midnight on Halloween and look over your left shoulder, you will see your future husband.

Bake small cakes with certain charms in them: a coin, a ring, a rag and a thimble. You can tell who will be rich, married, poor, or will earn her own living by who selects which cake.

On Halloween night, if you hold up a candle and look into a mirror, you will see the face of your future husband or wife.

Take three dishes and fill one with clear water, one with milky water, and leave the third one empty. Blindfold someone. If she touches the clear water, she will marry a bachelor. If she touches the milky water, she'll marry a widower. If she touches the empty one, she will not marry.

On Halloween, children would put corn meal by their beds to receive messages from ghosts written in the grain.

Fireside Cookout

...cool nights, a crackling fire, and friends

Velvety Ham and Cheese Chowder
Smothered Hot Dogs
Camper's Beans
Spicy Molasses Cookies
Hot Buttered Cider
Fireside Delight Chocolate Dip

*Listen! The wind is rising,
and the air is wild with leaves.
We have had our summer evenings,
now for October eves!*
- Humbert Wolfe

Baked Beans

Velvety Ham and Cheese Chowder

Serve in big, thick mugs with rye crackers.

1 large onion, chopped
1/2 t. butter
1 ham hock
3 baking potatoes, diced
1 t. dried or 2 t. fresh
    parsley, chopped

2 t. instant chicken broth
    granules
8 oz. box processed cheese,
    cubed
2 c. ham, cooked and cubed
1 pint half and half
8 oz. can succotash

Sauté onion in butter. In soup pot, place ham hock in water to cover. Add potatoes, onion and seasonings. Simmer for 20 minutes, then remove ham hock and mash potatoes into the liquid with a large spoon or potato masher. Add cheese and simmer until cheese is melted and soup is thickened. Add ham, cream and succotash. Simmer 10 additional minutes.

The true essentials of a feast are only fun and feed.
- Oliver Wendell Holmes

Smothered Hot Dogs

The longer they simmer, the better they taste.

1/2 small onion, minced
1 can beer
1 T. Worcestershire sauce

1/4 c. chili sauce
12 all beef hot dogs
12 hot dog buns

Mix all ingredients except hot dogs in a saucepan. Add hot dogs and simmer for 30 minutes, stirring occasionally. Serve dogs and sauce on buns.

Camper's Beans

For extra special beans, add a few chunks of hickory-smoked ham.

6-8 strips of bacon
1 small onion, chopped
1/4 c. brown sugar
2 t. vinegar

1/4 c. catsup
2 T. mustard
2-32 oz. cans of beans

Brown bacon to a crisp. While it is cooking, add onion to fat and let it brown. Drain bacon and onion and place on a paper towel. Break bacon into pieces. Combine brown sugar, vinegar, catsup and mustard in a large soup pan and cook over low heat 15 minutes. Add beans, bacon and onion and simmer, uncovered, at least 30 minutes, stirring occasionally.

Spicy Molasses Cookies

A real treat after your game of touch football!

3/4 c. soft shortening
1 c. brown sugar, packed
1 egg
1/4 c. molasses
1 t. cinnamon
2 1/4 c. flour

2 t. soda
1 t. ginger
1/2 t. cloves
1/4 t. salt
white sugar for dipping

Mix together shortening, brown sugar, egg and molasses. In separate bowl, stir together remaining dry ingredients except white sugar. Then mix dry ingredients into shortening mixture. Chill dough 2 hours or overnight. Roll dough into balls the size of large walnuts and dip tops in sugar. Place on lightly greased baking sheet about 3 inches apart, sugared side up. Bake in 375 degree oven about 10 to 12 minutes, until just set but not hard. Cool on wire rack. Makes 4 dozen.

Any occasion can be a celebration. Make the evening really fun and special...break out the sparklers!

Hot Buttered Cider

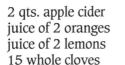

Aroma that fills the air on a cool fall evening.

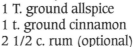

2 qts. apple cider	1 T. honey
juice of 2 oranges	1 T. ground allspice
juice of 2 lemons	1 t. ground cinnamon
15 whole cloves	2 1/2 c. rum (optional)
6 cinnamon sticks	3 T. butter

Simmer all ingredients (except butter) in a pot over the open fire for about 30 minutes. Strain if you like, stir in butter and serve hot.

Even an old boot tastes good if it is cooked over charcoal.

- Italian folk saying

Fireside Cookout

Fireside Delight Chocolate Dip

Try dipping toasted marshmallows into the rich,
velvety chocolate.

3 T. butter   2 c. sweetened cocoa mix
3 T. milk or water   1/4 t. instant coffee

Melt butter in small pan over campfire. Add milk, cocoa and coffee. Stir briskly with whisk or wooden spoon until hot, but not boiling. Add more milk or water if needed. With wooden skewers or fondue forks, dip slices of apples, bananas, peaches, pineapples, oranges, or angel food cake.

In the other gardens
And all up the vale,
From autumn bonfires
See the smoke trail!

Pleasant summer over
And all the summer flowers,
The red fire blazes,
The grey smoke towers.
—R.L. Stevenson

44

Creative cookouts...

Open Fire Orange Cakes

Hollow out some oranges by cutting the tops off, then scraping out most of the center with a sharp knife. It's o.k. if some of the orange is left inside...it will add to the flavor! Pour cake batter into the orange cups, filling them about half-full. Replace the lids, then wrap them in foil and bake over hot coals about 10 minutes, or until a toothpick comes out clean.

A fireside cookout can be as near as your own backyard or as far away as a mountain retreat. The point of it all is to join friends and family, rejoice in the crisp fall air, and bask in the beauty of the turning seasons. Be a kid again...play touch football, toast marshmallows, tell ghost stories...jump into a pile of leaves!

Peppermint Foot Bath

After a hike or a hard day, treat yourself to this pick-me-up for tired and aching feet. Gather several stems of fresh peppermint, or 2 ounces of dried peppermint leaves. Combine with about four ounces of juniper berries in a saucepan and add a quart of water. Heat slowly to just below boiling, stirring occasionally. Cover the pan let it sit until the mixture is just warm. Add 12 drops of sandalwood essential oil and 6 drops of cypress oil and stir. Strain through a coffee filter and pour the liquid into storage jars. When ready to use, fill a large pan or bowl with moderately hot water and stir in about 1/4 of the mixture. Soak feet for at least 10 minutes. Aaaah!

Pine Cone Candles

Collect pine cones during your autumn outing, and use them as a base for beautiful candles. Wrap candle wicking around the pine cones, tucking it in so it's securely wrapped, and leave an inch or so at the pointy end. Dip your pine cones several times in melted paraffin. If you have an assortment of candle stubs you've saved, you can also melt these to make interesting colors. Melt your wax in an old coffee can placed in a double boiler filled one third full with water, over very low heat. If you're making candles indoors, you can save on clean-up by using an electric skillet lined with foil and about 1/2" of water; then put your coffee can on top of the foil for a "double-boiler" effect and melt wax over low heat. To make the candles stand up, you can hold your dripping candles over muffin tins to create a round wax base. Your pine cone candles can also be used as firestarters, and look pretty in a basket by the fireplace or on the mantel.

Oktoberfest

...songs and laughter,
beer and brats

Hot Browned Pumpernickel Rounds
Grilled Sauerkraut Dogs
Cheddar Dogs
Sauerkraut Cream Cheese Loaf
Bavarian Apple Torte
Pickles & Relishes

O suns and skies and clouds of June,
And flowers of June together,
Ye cannot rival for one hour
October's bright blue weather.
- Helen Hunt Jackson

Hot Browned Pumpernickel Rounds

If you like hot flavor, add a bit of horseradish. Keep cold beer handy!

1 c. Swiss cheese, finely grated
4 slices bacon, cooked and crumbled
4 1/2 oz. can ripe olives, drained and chopped

1/4 c. green onions, minced
1 T. Worcestershire sauce
1/4 c. mayonnaise
large loaf of pumpernickel bread, sliced

Mix all ingredients except bread. Cut rounds of pumpernickel with a cookie cutter. Spread mixture on rounds and bake at 375 degrees for 10 to 15 minutes, or until browned.

(Note: remaining scraps of bread may be used to make delicious croutons or bread crumbs.)

Grilled Bratwurst and Sauerkraut

Have you ever had real bratwurst? They're heavenly with a bit of brown mustard; this recipe adds even more flavor.

1/4 c. sugar
2 T. vinegar
1 c. sauerkraut, drained and coarsely chopped
2 T. onion

2 T. green pepper, finely chopped
1 T. pimento, drained and diced
6 bratwursts

Combine sugar and vinegar and bring to a boil, stirring until sugar dissolves. Remove from heat and allow to cool. Combine sauerkraut, onion, green pepper and pimento. Add to vinegar mixture. Refrigerate 3 hours. Slit bratwursts almost in two. Drain sauerkraut mixture and spoon into the meat. Place on grill and cook until heated through. Serves 6.

Bratwurst and knockwurst are German sausages often braised in dark German beer. Just place the sausages in a pan with enough beer to halfway cover them. Bring the beer to a simmer and cook until it has evaporated. Then continue browning the sausages in the pan, or cook them on a hot grill.

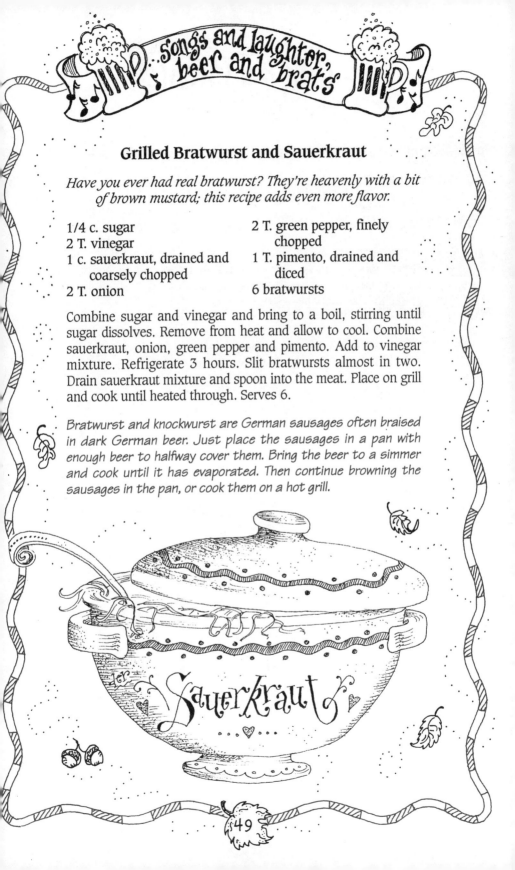

Sauerkraut

Cheddar Dogs

Kids love the melted cheese and bacon.

1/2 c. cheddar cheese, grated	2 T. tomato, chopped
4 slices bacon, cooked and crumbled	8 hot dogs

Combine cheese, bacon and tomato. Slit the hot dogs and spoon cheese mixture inside. Cook on grill until cheese is melted and hot dog is heated through. Serve on buns, or cut into bite-sized pieces for the little ones. Serves 8.

Make your favorite recipe for soft pretzels (see the "Tailgate" chapter for ours). Instead of making the typical twist shape, let the kids make pretzels in the shapes of their names or initials. Then sprinkle with coarse salt and bake as usual. Fun!

Sing a song of seasons!
Something bright in all!
Flowers in the summer,
Fires in the fall!
–Robert Louis Stevenson

Sauerkraut Cream Cheese Loaf

An attractive cold sauerkraut salad.

29 oz. can sauerkraut
2 c. sharp cheddar cheese, grated
2 T. onion, chopped
2 T. pimento, chopped
3 T. green pepper, chopped
1 hard boiled egg, chopped

1/4 c. mayonnaise
1/2 t. salt
1/2 c. bread crumbs
1 T. sugar
stuffed green olives, sliced
8 oz. pkg. cream cheese, softened

Drain sauerkraut and squeeze dry. Mix all ingredients except cream cheese. Shape into a loaf and chill overnight. Top with cream cheese "icing" and garnish with olives.

> The morns are meeker than they were,
> The nuts are getting brown;
> The berry's cheek is plumper,
> The rose is out of town.
>
> —Emily Dickinson

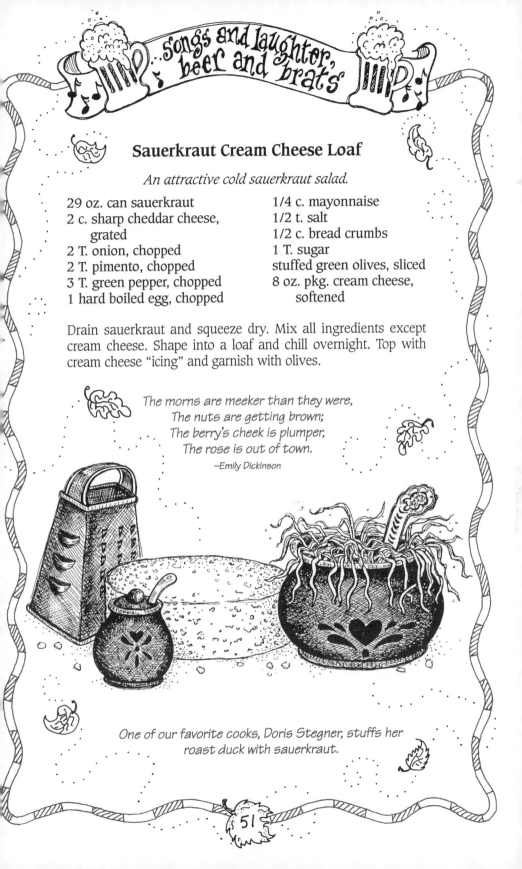

One of our favorite cooks, Doris Stegner, stuffs her roast duck with sauerkraut.

Bavarian Apple Torte

You may try this recipe with fresh pears, too! Since they're more delicate than apples, you'll want to sprinkle the sugar and cinnamon over them instead of tossing.

1/2 c. butter, softened
1/3 c. sugar
1/4 t. vanilla extract
1 c. flour
8 oz. pkg. cream cheese,
   softened
1/4 c. sugar

1 egg
1/2 t. vanilla extract
5 or 6 Jonathan apples,
   peeled and sliced
1/3 c. sugar
1/2 t. ground cinnamon
1/4 c. sliced almonds

Cream together butter and 1/3 cup sugar until light and fluffy. Blend in 1/4 teaspoon vanilla, add flour and mix well. Spread dough into a 9" square pan. Combine cream cheese and 1/4 cup sugar; mix well. Blend in egg and 1/2 teaspoon vanilla. Pour on top of dough. Toss apples with remaining 1/3 cup sugar and cinnamon. Spoon over cream cheese layer. Sprinkle with almonds. Bake at 450 degrees for 10 minutes. Reduce temperature to 400 degrees and bake 25 minutes longer. Allow to cool completely and cut into squares. Makes 12 servings.

What's Oktoberfest all about?

When the first German settlers came to America, they moved to Iowa and Wisconsin, and brought their love of beer brewing and sausage making with them.

In many Midwestern communities today, the third weekend in October is reserved for Oktoberfest...an autumn feast. The pigs are slaughtered for sausages, huge barrels are filled with batches of sauerkraut, the dark beer flows and the oompah bands march down the street.

A peck of pickles, mustards & relishes...

Homemade Pickles

Crunchy and sour...the real thing!

4 medium onions, sliced
10 cucumbers
2 1/2 t. dill seed
2 1/2 t. celery seed
1/4 plus 1/16 t. alum

4 c. sugar
1 qt. vinegar
1 qt. water
1/2 c. salt

Place 4 slices onion in the bottom of 5 sterilized canning jars. Cut cucumbers into quarters lengthwise; place in jars to fill. Add 1/2 teaspoon dill seed, 1/2 teaspoon celery seed and 1/16 teaspoon alum to each jar. In large saucepan combine sugar, vinegar, water and salt. Bring to a boil. Pour boiling liquid over cucumbers in each jar, leaving 1/2 inch at top; seal. Allow to stand for 2 weeks before using. Makes 5 quarts.

Display your jars of homemade pickles and mustards in a pretty windowbox, sparkling in the sunlight, all in a row.

Sweet 'n Hot Mustard

Serve with sausages, ham, hot dogs, or soft pretzels.

4 oz. can dry mustard
1 c. white wine vinegar
3 eggs, beaten
1 T. molasses

1 T. honey
3/4 c. sugar
1 T. whole mustard seed
2 c. mayonnaise

Mix dry mustard and vinegar; cover. Let stand for 8 hours or overnight. In medium saucepan, mix eggs, molasses, honey, sugar and mustard mixture. Stir over low heat until thickened, about 20 minutes; allow to cool. Add whole mustard seed and mayonnaise; cover and refrigerate. Makes 4 cups.

You can pickle just about anything in your garden...cauliflower, cabbage, carrots, beans, broccoli, onions and green tomatoes.

Pickled Beets

They're not only tasty...their deep red color makes the table look so pretty.

4 large beets, trimmed,
   cleaned and peeled
1 medium yellow onion,
   peeled and sliced
1 clove garlic, peeled and sliced

1 c. cider vinegar
1/4 c. sugar
1 T. cardamom seeds
1 T. whole cloves
pinch of salt

In a medium pan, cover the beets with cold water and bring the water just to a boil. Reduce heat and simmer, partially covered, 30 minutes, or until tender. Reserve about 2 cups of the cooking liquid. Slice the beets and put into a quart jar along with the sliced onion and garlic. In the reserved beet juice, add the vinegar, sugar and spices. Heat just enough to dissolve the sugar. Pour the mixture into the jar, over the beets. Allow to cool to room temperature; then cover and refrigerate at least 8 hours before serving.

Here's an idea for easy, quick pickled eggs...just add hard boiled eggs to a jar of pickled beets, either homemade or off the shelf. Store in the fridge for a few days. The eggs will absorb the beet juice...a great addition to your relish tray!

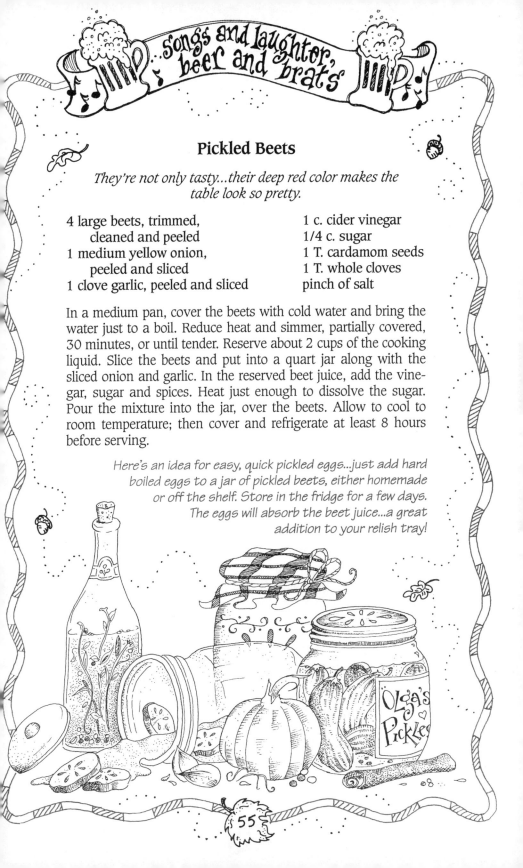

Oktoberfest

Garlic Dill Pickles

13 1/2 c. white vinegar
13 1/2 c. water
2 1/4 c. salt
1 1/2 c. pickling spices

10 lbs. cucumbers, 2 to 3"
    long, thoroughly cleaned
12 cloves garlic, peeled and
    minced
15 stems of fresh dill

Combine the vinegar, water, salt and spices into a brine and bring to a boil in a large pot. Fill sterilized 1-quart jars with the cucumbers, garlic and dill and cover with the hot brine. Leave 1/2" at the top of each jar. Wipe the rims carefully and seal the jars. (Follow the manufacturer's directions for processing the jars before canning.)

Note: For a really different pickle, try substituting fresh rosemary or tarragon for the dill.

Tomato Pepper Relish

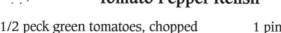

1/2 peck green tomatoes, chopped
8 red peppers, chopped
2 large onions, peeled and chopped
2 T. salt
1 pint white vinegar

1 pint sugar
2 sticks cinnamon
2 T. whole allspice
2 T. whole cloves
1 T. celery seeds

Boil the vegetables for 15 minutes. Remove from heat and add the salt. Bring to boil again and simmer for 15 minutes. Drain the vegetables and return to the pan. Then add the vinegar, sugar, cinnamon, allspice and cloves. Bring to a rapid boil, then add the celery seeds. Pour into jars and seal.

Come for Soup

...hearty soups and heavenly breads

The Soups...

French Onion Soup with Toasted Rye and Gruyere
Vegetable Stew
Mediterranean Peasant Soup
Potato-Cheddar Chowder
Burgundy Beef Stew
Italian Wedding Soup
Cream of Broccoli Soup
Black Bean Soup
Basic Chicken Stock
Chicken Soup with Wild Rice and Mushrooms
Split Pea Soup with Ham
New England Lobster Stew

The Breads...

Cheddar Cheese Spoon Bread
Three-Grain Amish Bread
Crusty Cornmeal Rolls
Caraway Rye Bread
Ripe Olive Bread
Little Bread Cups

Of soup and love, the first is best.
- Spanish Proverb

Come for Soup

French Onion Soup with Toasted Rye and Gruyere

Sweet, tender onions in a rich broth, smothered under a canopy of crusty bread and melted cheese.

4 T. sweet butter
4 large Vidalia onions, halved and thinly sliced
1/4 c. sugar
salt and pepper to taste

3-16 oz. cans beef broth (or 6 c. homemade beef stock)
2 T. port wine or sherry
4 thick slices rye bread, toasted
1 c. Gruyere cheese, grated

In a large soup pot, melt the butter and cook the onions, covered, over low heat for 20 minutes. Stir the onions occasionally. When the onions are soft and transparent, sprinkle the sugar over them and stir the onions, cooking uncovered about 10 minutes, or until onions are brown and caramelized. Add salt and pepper to taste. Add half of the beef stock and simmer, uncovered, 15 minutes. Add the remaining stock and the wine and cook another 30 to 40 minutes. Fill four ovenproof soup bowls and put a slice of toasted rye bread on top of each. Divide the cheese among the four bowls, sprinkling on top of the bread. Place the soups bowls on a baking sheet under a preheated broiler and broil just until the cheese melts. Serves 4.

Vegetable Stew

A hearty, satisfying way to eat your vegetables.

3 slices bacon
4 T. unsalted butter
1 1/2 c. onions, chopped
4 c. leeks, tough green leaves removed, sliced
6 c. chicken stock or broth
2 carrots, washed and sliced
3 stalks celery, sliced

1 t. dried tarragon
1/2 t. dried thyme
salt and pepper to taste
4 c. potatoes, peeled and chopped
1 lb. spinach, washed and cut up
1/2 c. whipping cream

In a large soup pot, cook the bacon over medium-high heat until crisp. Remove bacon and set aside. Lower the heat and add butter. Add onions and leeks to the pot and cook until softened. Pour in chicken broth. Add carrots, celery, seasonings and potatoes. Simmer, covered, until potatoes are tender, about 20 minutes. Add the spinach and simmer for another minute. Remove the soup from heat. Put half the soup in a food processor and puree. Return the pureed soup to the pot. Add the remaining spinach and the cream. Heat thoroughly, taste, and add seasonings if desired. Ladle into bowls and garnish with crumbled bacon. Serves 8.

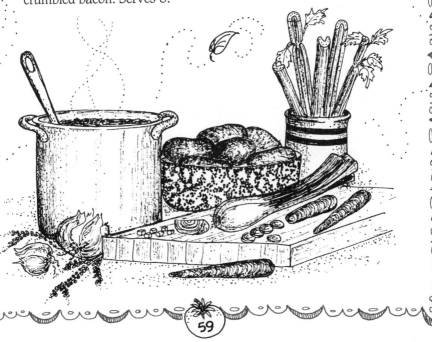

Mediterranean Peasant Soup

Experiment with different types of day-old bread: garlic, olive, or sundried tomato.

3 cloves garlic, crushed
1/4 c. olive oil
4 ripe tomatoes, peeled and
   chopped
6 c. beef broth
3 T. fresh basil, chopped

1/8 t. ground red pepper
salt and pepper to taste
6 thick slices crusty white
   bread, toasted*
1/3 c. Romano cheese,
   freshly grated

In a large saucepan sauté garlic in heated olive oil until tender. Add tomatoes and sauté 5 minutes. Add broth and seasonings and bring to a boil. Immediately reduce heat and simmer, covered, about 25 minutes. Break bread into bite-sized pieces and divide among 6 bowls. Pour soup over bread and sprinkle with cheese.

If you love garlic, rub slices of Italian bread with garlic before you toast them.

Potato-Cheddar Chowder

The beer adds a hearty malt flavor to this creamy, rich soup.

1/4 lb. sweet butter
1 carrot, diced
1 stalk celery, diced
3 scallions, thinly sliced
4 white potatoes, peeled and
   cubed
1/2 c. all-purpose flour
4 c. chicken broth or stock
1 can beer or ale

1 c. Parmesan cheese, freshly
   grated
1/2 lb. sharp Cheddar cheese,
   grated
1/2 lb. white Cheddar cheese,
   grated
salt and pepper to taste
red and/or green bell pepper,
   diced, for garnish
1/2 t. dried dill, for garnish

In a heavy pot, melt the butter over low heat. Add all of the vegetables and the flour, and cook, stirring every so often, for 5 minutes. Add the broth and the beer and simmer, continuing to stir. With a wire whisk, blend in the three cheeses and the seasonings. Simmer over low heat for about 10 minutes, but do not boil. Serve in a tureen or individual bowls, garnished with the peppers and a sprinkle of dill. Serves 8.

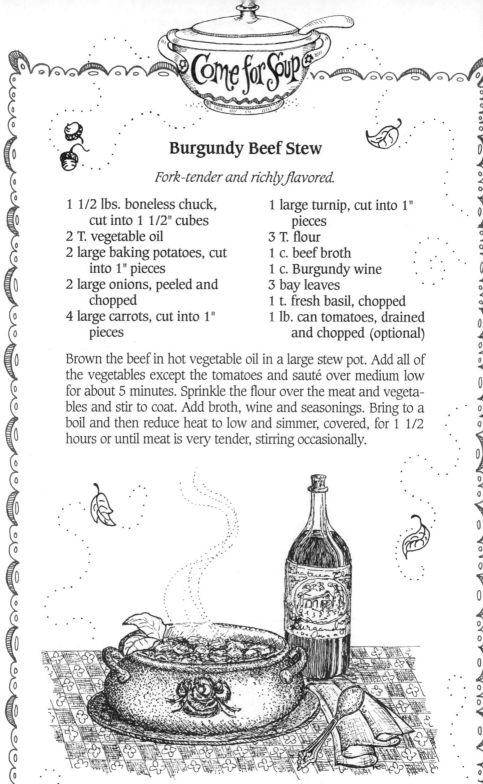

Burgundy Beef Stew

Fork-tender and richly flavored.

1 1/2 lbs. boneless chuck, cut into 1 1/2" cubes
2 T. vegetable oil
2 large baking potatoes, cut into 1" pieces
2 large onions, peeled and chopped
4 large carrots, cut into 1" pieces

1 large turnip, cut into 1" pieces
3 T. flour
1 c. beef broth
1 c. Burgundy wine
3 bay leaves
1 t. fresh basil, chopped
1 lb. can tomatoes, drained and chopped (optional)

Brown the beef in hot vegetable oil in a large stew pot. Add all of the vegetables except the tomatoes and sauté over medium low for about 5 minutes. Sprinkle the flour over the meat and vegetables and stir to coat. Add broth, wine and seasonings. Bring to a boil and then reduce heat to low and simmer, covered, for 1 1/2 hours or until meat is very tender, stirring occasionally.

Italian Wedding Soup

This is the traditional festive soup with little meatballs.

1 lb. ground beef
1 lb. ground sausage
2 eggs
1 c. soft bread crumbs
2 t. oregano
1 t. rosemary
1 clove garlic, crushed
olive oil
2-15 oz. cans chicken broth
2 cans water

5 oz. pkg. vermicelli
　　pasta
1 c. fresh spinach leaves,
　　torn into pieces
1 large onion, sliced fine
6 mushrooms, thinly sliced
2 eggs, lightly beaten
Parmesan cheese, freshly
　　grated

In a large bowl, combine beef, sausage, eggs, bread crumbs, oregano, rosemary and garlic. Shape mixture into bite-sized meatballs. Gently and evenly, brown the meatballs in olive oil until cooked; drain the skillet and set aside. In a large saucepan, combine broth and water and bring to a boil. Add pasta, meatballs and spinach. Simmer, uncovered, until noodles are tender. Add the onion and mushrooms and drop in the eggs, stirring only until the eggs are cooked. Remove from heat. Sprinkle individual portions with Parmesan cheese. Serves 10.

Come for Soup

Cream of Broccoli Soup

Indulge by adding a pat of butter to your bowl.

1 large carrot, chopped
1 stalk celery, chopped
1 onion, peeled and chopped
1 potato, peeled and finely
   chopped

4 c. chicken stock
1 large head broccoli, cut in
   flowerets and chopped
1 1/2 c. half and half, scalded
salt and pepper to taste

Combine all vegetables except the broccoli with the chicken stock in a saucepan and bring to a boil. Reduce heat and simmer, covered, 20 minutes or until tender. Meanwhile, cook the broccoli in another pan or in the microwave until tender. Transfer soup and half the broccoli into a food processor and blend until smooth. Return soup to the pan and blend in the half and half and the remaining broccoli. Bring to serving temperature and season with salt and pepper. Serves 8.

Beautiful soup, so rich and green,
Waiting in a hot tureen!
Who for such dainties
would not stoop?
Soup of the evening,
beautiful soup!

\- Lewis Carroll

Black Bean Soup

Hearty, healthful flavor on a blustery fall day.

1 lb. dry black beans
2 1/2 qts. water
4 strips bacon, cut into small
  pieces
1 stalk celery, chopped
2 medium onions, chopped
2 T. flour
2 smoked ham hocks, split,
  or 1 ham bone
3 sprigs parsley

2 bay leaves
2 cloves garlic, chopped
2 carrots, chopped
salt and freshly ground
  pepper to taste
1/2 c. Madeira wine
Garnish:
1/2 c. sour cream
  and minced scallions

Wash beans, cover with cold water and soak 8 hours or overnight. Drain and rinse. Place in a large pot and add the water. Cover and simmer 1 1/2 hours. In a Dutch oven, brown bacon and drain most of fat. Add celery and onion and cook just until tender. Blend in flour and cook, stirring, about a minute. Add ham, parsley, bay leaves, garlic, carrots, seasonings and beans, including cooking liquid. Cover and simmer over low heat, stirring occasionally, for three or four hours. Add water if necessary. Remove any bones from soup; remove ham, chop fine and set aside. Transfer half of soup to blender, blend and return to soup. Return ham to soup. Add wine and mix well. Garnish each portion with a dollop of sour cream and minced scallions. Serves 8.

Basic Chicken Stock

Make ahead and freeze 'til you need it. Used in so many recipes...so much more flavorful than canned chicken broth.

bones from 1 whole chicken*
2 carrots, scrubbed and cut into
    chunks
4 stalks celery, including leaves,
    cut into chunks
1 onion, peeled

4 cloves
2 sprigs fresh parsley
1 t. dried thyme
5 black peppercorns
1 T. fresh lemon juice
2 bay leaves

Place all ingredients into a large stockpot and cover with 4 quarts of cold water. Bring the water to a boil, reduce heat and skim the top by moving the pot slightly off the burner. (The fat will travel to the cooler part of the pot.) Simmer, uncovered, about 2 1/2 hours. Strain the liquid, chill, and remove the fat. Makes about 1 quart.

After you've enjoyed your Sunday roast chicken, save the bones for your stockpot!

Chicken Soup with Wild Rice and Mushrooms

If you want to make this into a creamy soup, just add 1/2 cup cream along with the wine.

2 T. butter
2 c. onions, peeled and diced
2 c. carrots, diced
2 c. celery, diced
2 cloves garlic, peeled and
    diced
1 c. wild rice
8 c. chicken stock (see recipe
    above)

2 bay leaves
1 t. dried thyme
1/2 c. white wine
2 c. cooked chicken (white
    and dark meat)
2 c. fresh mushrooms,
    cleaned and sliced
salt and pepper to taste
fresh parsley for garnish

Melt the butter in a large soup pot and add the onions, carrots, celery and garlic. Sauté until soft. Add the rice, stock, bay leaves and thyme. Simmer, covered, for one hour. Add the wine, chicken, mushrooms and seasonings. Garnish with chopped fresh parsley.

Split Pea Soup with Ham

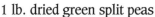

Meaty and satisfying; the spinach adds a rich flavor to the broth.

1 lb. dried green split peas
5 c. chicken stock or broth
5 c. water
1 ham bone with meat, or 2 smoked ham hocks
2 stalks celery with leaves, diced
3 T. fresh parsley, chopped

1/2 t. dried tarragon
4 T. sweet butter
1 c. carrots, peeled and diced
1 c. onion, diced
1 c. fresh spinach, finely chopped
freshly ground pepper to taste

Rinse the peas. Combine stock and water in a large pot and add the peas; bring to a boil. Add the ham bone, celery, parsley and tarragon. Reduce heat and simmer, partially covered, about 45 minutes. In a separate pan, melt the butter and sauté the carrots and onion until soft. Add to the soup. Stir in the spinach and simmer, partially covered, 30 minutes. Remove the ham bone and, with a fork, remove meat from the bone. Return the ham to the soup. Season to taste. Serves 6.

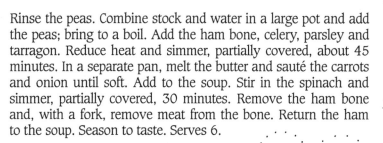

Only the pure of heart can make a good soup.
- Ludwig Van Beethoven

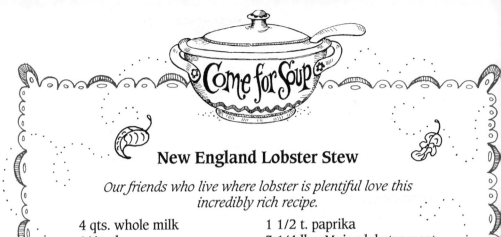

Come for Soup

New England Lobster Stew

Our friends who live where lobster is plentiful love this incredibly rich recipe.

4 qts. whole milk
1/4 c. heavy cream
1/4 c. sweet butter, melted

1 1/2 t. paprika
3 1/4 lbs. Maine lobster meat
pinch of salt

Heat the milk and cream in a double boiler; do not allow to boil. In an iron skillet, combine the melted butter and paprika. Heat slowly to make a sauce. Add the lobster and heat slowly, gently warming the meat (do not overheat). Add the lobster mixture to the hot milk and heat gently for an hour. Add a bit of salt if desired. Tastes even better if refrigerated and reheated the next day. Serve with oyster crackers. Serves 8.

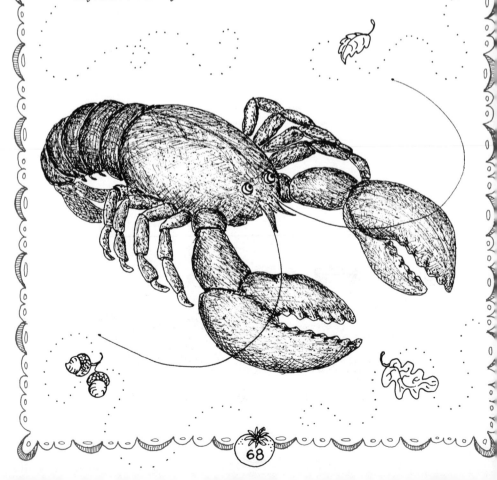

Ideas to bowl them over...

Try serving soups and chowders in these creative containers!
Butternut squash...just cut in half, remove seeds and fibers, and
cook in the microwave.

Bell peppers make lovely soup cups. Make sure you select peppers that will stand up. If you like, vary the colors of red, green
and yellow. After you remove the seeds and membranes, fill the
raw peppers and replace the tops to keep the soup hot.

Little rye or sourdough bread rounds can be scooped out and
brushed with olive oil. Brown in a 350 degree oven about 10
minutes, then fill the loaves. Garnish with croutons made from
the leftover bread.

Special Soup Garnishes:
Toasted nuts
Paprika
Cooked, crumbled bacon
Slices or zest of lemon or lime
Sour cream
Matchstick carrots
Diced green onions
Paper-thin bell pepper rings
Tortilla chips
Rye, sourdough or whole wheat herbed croutons
Shredded cheese
Fresh parsley or dill

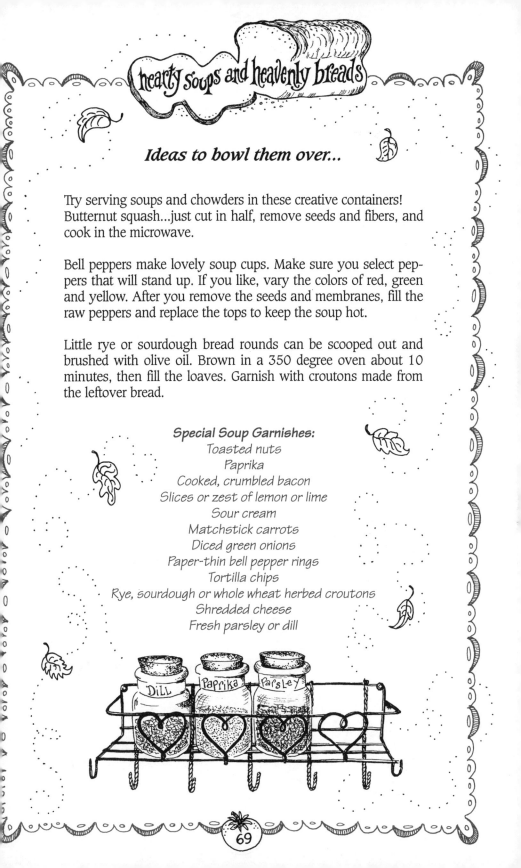

Come for Soup

Three-Grain Amish Bread

2 c. stone ground whole
    wheat flour
2 c. rye flour
2 c. unbleached white flour
1 qt. buttermilk
2 T. brown sugar

2 T. molasses
1/2 t. salt
2 rounded T. active dry yeast
1 c. warm water
1 t. brown sugar
3/4 c. shortening, melted

Mix the flours together in a large bowl. Heat the buttermilk to very warm, but not hot, and pour it into a separate bowl. Add the 2 tablespoons of brown sugar, molasses and salt, stirring until dissolved. Dissolve the yeast in the warm water; then add the teaspoon of brown sugar. When the yeast begins to bubble, add it to the buttermilk mixture. Gradually add some of the flour to the liquid, making a stiff batter. Then add the shortening and beat the dough until it is smooth. Allow the dough to rise for 12 minutes. After the dough has risen, add more flour to form a workable bread dough. Form into three loaves. Bake in a 350 degree oven for about an hour, testing for doneness.

To test bread for doneness, thump the crust with your finger. If it sounds hollow, it's done.

Cheddar Cheese Spoon Bread

A delicious companion to soup or chowder.

2 1/4 c. water
1 t. salt
1 c. cornmeal
1/2 t. pepper
1 T. butter

1 c. whole milk
4 large eggs, well beaten
1 1/2 c. sharp cheddar
   cheese, shredded
3 T. scallions, chopped

In a large saucepan, boil the water, add salt and lower heat to simmering. Add the cornmeal while stirring with a wire whisk and continue to cook, stirring constantly, for about 2 minutes or until mixture is smooth. Remove from the heat and whisk in pepper, butter and milk. When mixture is smooth, add the eggs and beat with the whisk. Stir in the cheese and scallions. Pour the mixture into a buttered 2-quart casserole and bake at 400 degrees for 40 minutes, or until a toothpick comes out clean. Serves 6 to 8.

Before the introduction of coins, the Egyptians gave loaves of bread as payment for their debts. (This gave new meaning to the word "dough"!)

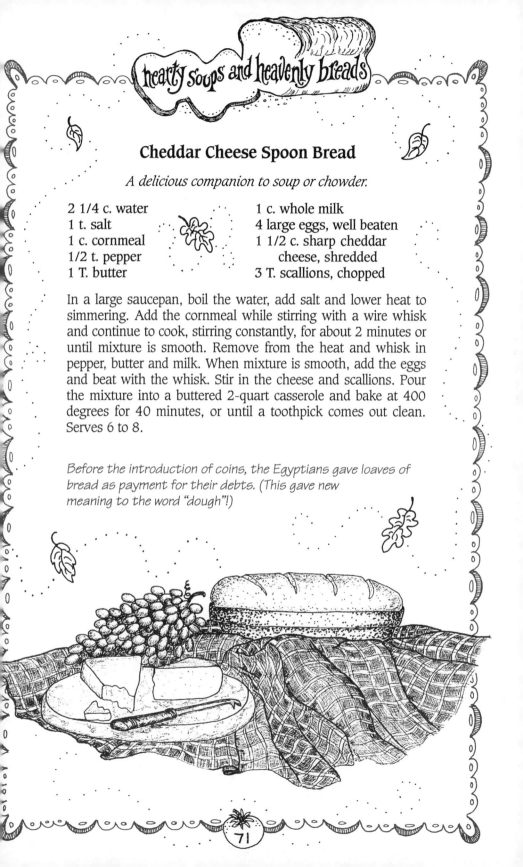

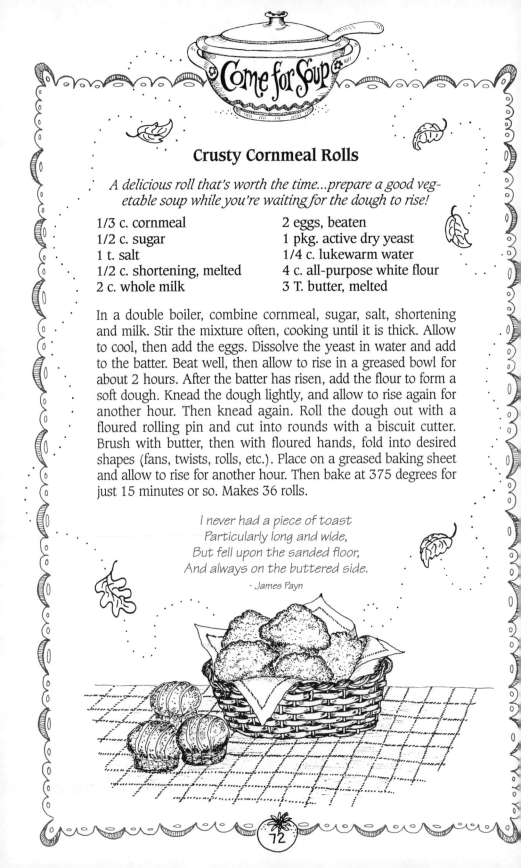

Crusty Cornmeal Rolls

A delicious roll that's worth the time...prepare a good veg-etable soup while you're waiting for the dough to rise!

1/3 c. cornmeal
1/2 c. sugar
1 t. salt
1/2 c. shortening, melted
2 c. whole milk

2 eggs, beaten
1 pkg. active dry yeast
1/4 c. lukewarm water
4 c. all-purpose white flour
3 T. butter, melted

In a double boiler, combine cornmeal, sugar, salt, shortening and milk. Stir the mixture often, cooking until it is thick. Allow to cool, then add the eggs. Dissolve the yeast in water and add to the batter. Beat well, then allow to rise in a greased bowl for about 2 hours. After the batter has risen, add the flour to form a soft dough. Knead the dough lightly, and allow to rise again for another hour. Then knead again. Roll the dough out with a floured rolling pin and cut into rounds with a biscuit cutter. Brush with butter, then with floured hands, fold into desired shapes (fans, twists, rolls, etc.). Place on a greased baking sheet and allow to rise for another hour. Then bake at 375 degrees for just 15 minutes or so. Makes 36 rolls.

I never had a piece of toast
Particularly long and wide,
But fell upon the sanded floor,
And always on the buttered side.

- James Payn

Caraway Rye Bread

Try this delicious bread with black bean or French onion soup.

1 pkg. active dry yeast
3/4 c. plus 2 T. warm water,
    divided
1/4 t. sugar
2 c. all-purpose flour
1 c. rye flour
1 T. caraway seeds
1 t. salt

2 T. vegetable oil
1 T. honey
2 T. cornmeal
1 egg, beaten with 1 T. water
caraway seeds
1/2 t. black pepper, freshly
    ground

Combine the yeast with 3/4 cup water and sugar and set aside until yeast bubbles. Stir together the flours, caraway seeds and salt in a large bowl. Add the yeast, oil, honey, and 2 tablespoons warm water, stirring until a ball of dough is formed. If the dough is too stiff, add a few drops of water. Knead with floured hands on a floured surface for about 10 minutes. Place the dough in a large oiled bowl, cover loosely and allow to rise in a sink of warm water about 45 minutes. Dough should double in size. Punch it down and shape it into a ball, return to the bowl and let it rise another 30 minutes. Sprinkle the cornmeal onto a lightly buttered baking sheet. Punch your dough down and form it into a loaf. Place it on the baking sheet, cover with a clean towel, and allow to rise another 30 minutes, or until doubled again. Brush the beaten egg over the loaf; then sprinkle with caraway seeds and freshly ground pepper. Cut several slashes across the top of the loaf. Bake in a 375 degree preheated oven about 35 minutes, or until golden brown. The bread should sound hollow when thumped with your finger. Let it cool on a wire rack.

Be creative with shapes when making yeast breads...for a special occasion, make a wreath-shaped bread. Portion part of the dough to form shapes such as leaves, flowers and berries to stick on top of the wreath. Then glaze with an egg wash before baking.

Ripe Olive Bread

They'll think you spent the day baking this quick, easy bread!

2 eggs	1 c. ripe black olives, drained
1 T. sugar	and chopped
1/2 t. salt	1 c. all-purpose flour
1/4 c. olive oil	2 t. baking soda
1/2 c. milk	

In a large bowl, beat the eggs, sugar, salt, oil and milk. Add the olives. Stir together the flour and baking powder and add to the egg mixture, stirring just until blended. Do not overbeat. Pour into a greased 8 1/2" x 4 1/2" x 2 1/2" loaf pan. Bake at 350 degrees for about one hour, or until a toothpick comes out clean. Remove loaf from the pan after it has cooled for 10 minutes and allow to cool completely.

Little Bread Cups

Fun to serve on the side...fill with soup garnishes such as cheese, croutons, fresh chives and sour cream.

12 slices white bread	fresh herbs of your choice
3 T. olive oil	

Trim crusts from the bread and flatten with a rolling pin. Press flattened bread slices into the cups of a muffin tin, trimming excess bread with a sharp knife. Brush each bread cup with olive oil. Sprinkle with dill, parsley, tarragon or garlic powder. Bake in a preheated 425 degree oven for about 10 minutes, or until crisp. Allow to cool for a few minutes before removing from muffin tin.

*Without bread,
without wine,
love is nothing.*
- French proverb

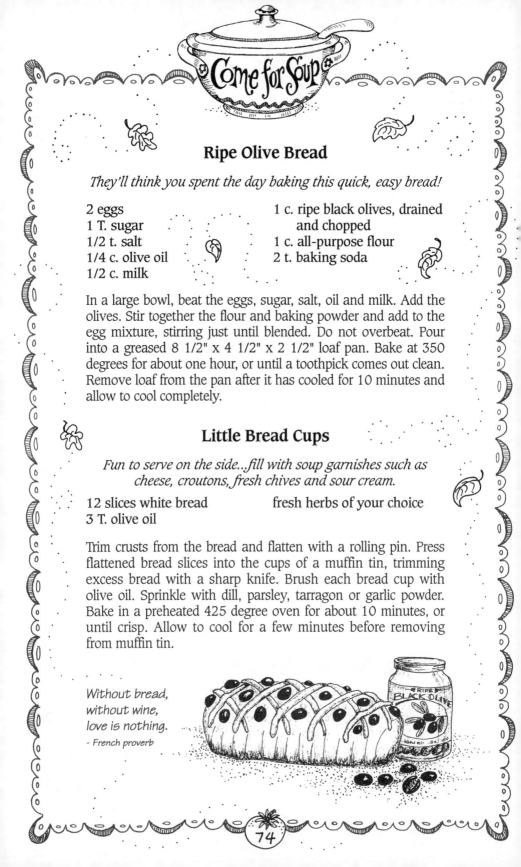

Apple Festival

...juicy recipes to celebrate the apple season

Apple-Cheddar Triple Loaves
Sausage Stuffed Apples
Pork Cutlets with Spiced Apples
Grilled Chicken Salad with Apple Dressing
Yam and Apple Bake
Apple Crunch Muffins
Jewish Apple Cake with Warm Cider Sauce
Paper Bag Apple Pie
Apple Butter
Mulled Cider

*...apples so red hang overhead,
and nuts, ripe-brown, come showering down
in the bountiful days of September!*
- Mary Howitt

Apple Festival

Apple-Cheddar Triple Loaves

Apples and cheddar cheese go together...it's as simple as that!

3 c. all-purpose flour
1/2 c. sugar
2 T. baking powder
3/4 t. salt
1 egg, beaten

1 egg yolk, beaten
1 1/2 c. milk
1/2 c. cooking oil
3/4 c. apples, diced
3/4 c. cheddar
    cheese, shredded

Combine flour, sugar, baking powder, and salt in a large mixing bowl. Combine the whole egg, egg yolk, milk and oil in a medium bowl; add to flour mixture and stir just until moistened. Gently fold in the apples and cheese. Divide batter among three greased 7 1/2" x 3 1/2" x 2" loaf pans. Bake at 350 degrees about 40 minutes, until inserted toothpick comes out clean. Cool 10 minutes and remove from pans. When completely cool, wrap in plastic wrap and store in refrigerator.

Fragrant herbs in terra cotta pots add aroma and color to your autumn kitchen.

Sausage-Stuffed Apples

Serve on a big platter surrounded by dollops of chunky applesauce sprinkled with walnuts and cinnamon.

4 medium red delicious
   apples
1 t. lemon juice
5 little sausage links,
   browned, drained and
   crumbled
1 c. cooked brown rice
1 T. onion, diced

1 t. celery, diced
3 oz. sharp cheddar cheese,
   cubed
1 T. walnuts, chopped
1 T. raisins
2 egg whites, lightly beaten
1/4 t. allspice
salt and pepper to taste

Core apples, leaving the bottoms intact. Hollow out the center of each apple, leaving the sides thick enough to hold together when cooked. Peel each apple halfway down and rub with lemon juice. Set aside. Mix all remaining ingredients together and stuff apples firmly with mixture. (If apples do not stand up, trim the bottoms to flatten.) Bake in a 375 degree oven for 15 minutes, or until golden brown.

If you've never been apple-picking, go...it's a memorable family outing. Children are amazed to see rows upon rows of stocky apple trees, laden with fat, juicy fruit. Many of the branches are well within a child's reach, and many of the ripe apples are just the right size for little ones. You won't find that hard, waxy texture on an apple right off the tree, either. Take a picnic lunch and make a day of it, with freshly picked apples for dessert.

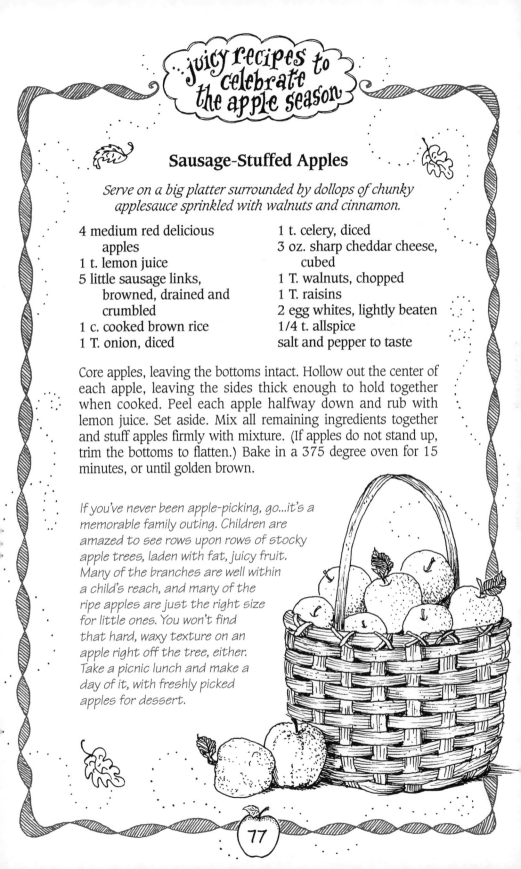

Pork Cutlets with Spiced Apples

Delicious with German potato salad on the side.

3 apples, cored and sliced
1/3 c. lemon juice
12 boneless pork loin cutlets,
   1/4" thick
2 T. butter

1 T. olive oil
2 oz. fresh ginger, cut into
   julienne strips
1/2 t. dried thyme, crushed
salt and pepper to taste

Toss apples with lemon juice. Cook pork in hot butter and oil for 5 minutes. Add apples, ginger, and thyme. Turn pork and cook 4 minutes longer. Add 1 tablespoon water, cover and simmer on low heat 5 minutes. Season with salt and pepper.

Grilled Chicken Salad with Apple Dressing

A really different dressing for chicken on the grill.

1/2 c. apple juice
1 c. apple, peeled and
   chopped
1 T. apple cider vinegar
1 t. cornstarch
1 lb. mixed salad greens

1/4 c. sliced almonds, toasted
1/2 c. cheddar cheese,
   shredded
1/2 c. red bell pepper, sliced
3/4 c. blue cheese, crumbled
12 oz. boneless, skinless
   chicken breasts, grilled

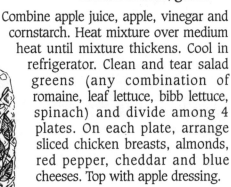

Combine apple juice, apple, vinegar and cornstarch. Heat mixture over medium heat until mixture thickens. Cool in refrigerator. Clean and tear salad greens (any combination of romaine, leaf lettuce, bibb lettuce, spinach) and divide among 4 plates. On each plate, arrange sliced chicken breasts, almonds, red pepper, cheddar and blue cheeses. Top with apple dressing.

...juicy recipes to celebrate the apple season

Yam and Apple Bake

Every year, Vickie's family insists she bring this dish for Thanksgiving!

6-8 yams
6-8 yellow delicious apples
1 c. granulated sugar
1/4 c. cornstarch

1 t. salt
2 c. boiling water
1/2 c. butter

Parboil yams, peel and cut into pieces. Pare apples and slice. Mix sugar, cornstarch and salt in saucepan. Add boiling water and butter, stir over medium heat until mixture comes to a boil. Butter casserole dish and place yams and apples in casserole in layers. Pour sauce over. Bake at 350 degrees for 1 hour.

The friendly cow all red and white,
I love with all my heart:
She gives me cream with all her might,
To eat with apple-tart.

    —Robert Louis Stevenson

Apple Festival

Apple Crunch Muffins

A delicious fall treat for breakfast on the run!

1 1/2 c. sifted flour	1 1/4 c. shortening
1/2 c. sugar	1 egg, slightly beaten
2 t. baking powder	1/2 c. milk
1/2 t. salt	1 c. Granny Smith apples, diced
1/2 t. cinnamon	

Topping:

1/4 c. brown sugar, packed	1/2 t. cinnamon
1/4 c. walnuts, chopped	

Mix these ingredients together to make topping.

Sift flour, sugar, baking powder, salt and cinnamon in mixing bowl. Cut in shortening until fine crumbs form. Combine milk and egg. Add to dry ingredients along with apples. Stir just to moisten. Spoon batter into muffin cups, filling 2/3 full. Sprinkle with brown sugar topping. Bake at 375 degrees for 25 minutes, or until golden brown. Makes 12.

Float perfect apples and cinnamon sticks in a big glass bowl of cider and arrange fresh grapes and greenery around the outside...makes a lovely presentation.

Jewish Apple Cake

The perfect cake for coffee and tea parties.

2 c. flour, sifted
2 c. sugar
3 t. baking powder
4 eggs, lightly beaten
1 c. vegetable oil
1/2 c. frozen orange juice
   concentrate, thawed and
   undiluted

2 1/2 t. vanilla extract
2-3 apples, peeled, cored,
   and chopped
4 T. sugar
2 t. ground cinnamon
Garnish: confectioner's
   sugar and slivered
   almonds

Preheat oven to 350 degrees. Combine all but the apples, sugar and cinnamon. In separate bowl, toss the apples with the sugar and cinnamon. Grease and flour a large tube pan. Pour in half the batter, and layer half the apple mixture over it. Add the rest of the batter, and top with the remaining apples. Bake for 75 minutes. Allow cake to cool for an hour before removing from pan. Sprinkle with confectioner's sugar and slivered almonds.

Warm Cider Sauce

Keep in the fridge for all kinds of desserts.

1 c. apple cider
3/4 c. light corn syrup
1/4 c. sugar
1/4 c. butter

juice and grated rind of 1
   lemon
1/2 t. nutmeg
pinch of ginger

Heat all ingredients together until sugar dissolves. Serve warm on top of apple cake, vanilla ice cream, pumpkin pie or apple dumplings.

A harvest display of gourds, pears, apples and bittersweet, arranged in a big wooden bowl will look warm and beautiful on your dining table.

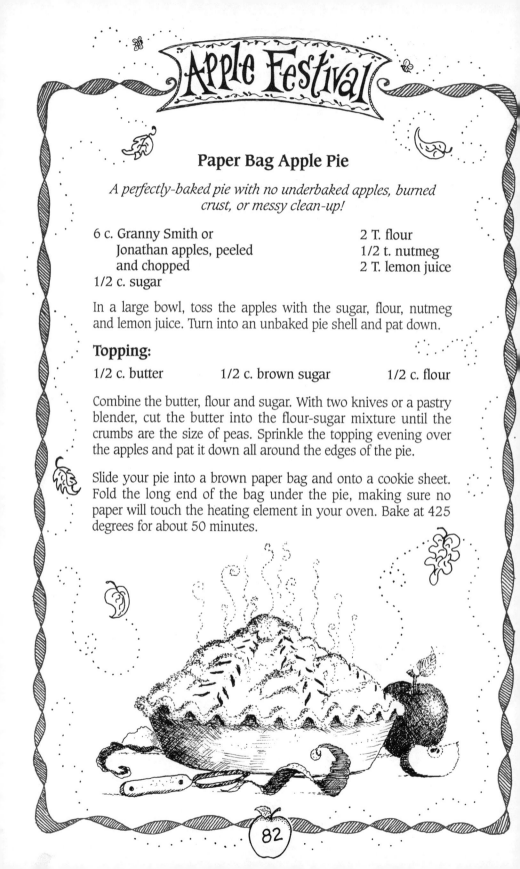

Apple Festival

Paper Bag Apple Pie

A perfectly-baked pie with no underbaked apples, burned crust, or messy clean-up!

6 c. Granny Smith or
   Jonathan apples, peeled
   and chopped
1/2 c. sugar

2 T. flour
1/2 t. nutmeg
2 T. lemon juice

In a large bowl, toss the apples with the sugar, flour, nutmeg and lemon juice. Turn into an unbaked pie shell and pat down.

Topping:

1/2 c. butter   1/2 c. brown sugar   1/2 c. flour

Combine the butter, flour and sugar. With two knives or a pastry blender, cut the butter into the flour-sugar mixture until the crumbs are the size of peas. Sprinkle the topping evening over the apples and pat it down all around the edges of the pie.

Slide your pie into a brown paper bag and onto a cookie sheet. Fold the long end of the bag under the pie, making sure no paper will touch the heating element in your oven. Bake at 425 degrees for about 50 minutes.

Apple Butter

Your whole house will be filled with an irresistible, spicy aroma.
Enough to last the whole year through,
or to give as holiday gifts!

10 lbs. (30 c.) tart apples,
   cored and sliced
5 c. apple cider
4 c. sugar

1 c. dark corn syrup
2 t. ground cinnamon
4 t. ground cloves

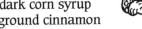

Place sliced apples in a 10-quart Dutch oven; add cider. Bring to a boil, then reduce heat and simmer about 30 minutes, or until apples are soft, stirring occasionally. Press apple mixture through a food mill or sieve; then return sieved apples to the Dutch oven. Allow mixture to boil gently, uncovered, for 30 minutes, remembering to stir occasionally. Add sugar and syrup and boil gently, stirring frequently with long-handled spoon, 3 to 4 hours or until desired thickness. Stir in cinnamon and cloves and cook 15 minutes more. Pour into 12 hot, clean half-pint jars, leaving 1/2 inch at the top. Wipe rims, adjust lids and process in boiling water bath for 10 minutes.

An apple pie without some cheese is like a kiss without a squeeze.

- Anonymous

Apple Peelin' Parties

In the northern part of the Midwest, apple harvest time was a good time to have a party. Guests would be assigned their own crock of apples to peel and core. Bachelors would compete to see who would finish the most apples...the winner was allowed to kiss any girl he chose! After the "peelin'," the parlor would be cleared out for dancing. They'd sprinkle cornmeal on the floor and a fiddler would tune up for square dancing. The next day, the ladies would return for the "stirrin'," and big copper kettles were placed on a log fire. They'd add scrubbed stones to keep the butter from scorching. Any apple butter than wasn't canned for the winter was kept frozen out on the back porch. Whenever anyone needed a taste of apple butter, they'd chip a piece out of the cask to thaw.

Mulled Cider

Try cider instead of coffee once in awhile...cut down on caffeine and enjoy the pure taste of fall!

2 qts. apple juice or sweet cider
1/2 c. light brown sugar, firmly packed
2-inch cinnamon stick

1 t. whole allspice
1 t. whole cloves
long cinnamon sticks

Mix apple juice or cider and sugar in large saucepan. Add spices. Heat mixture slowly to simmering. Cover pan, simmer 20 minutes, and strain. Serve hot, with a cinnamon stick in each mug.

Autumn treasures...

Preserved Leaves

Gather bright leaves and branches of scarlet, orange and red. In a jar, mix one part liquid glycerine (available at most drugstores) with three parts hot tap water. Pound the ends of the leaves and branches with a lightweight hammer, making it easier for them to absorb water. Stick the ends of the branches and leaves into the water-glycerine mixture. Allow to stand for about a week. The leaves will become soft and pliable. They are now preserved for wreaths and decorations.

Another method is to iron the leaves with waxed paper. Just preheat your iron to medium. On an ironing board, layer an old sheet or some newspaper first, to protect the surface. Then layer a sheet of waxed paper and top with leaves. Follow with another sheet of waxed paper. Put a piece of newspaper on the very top. Hold your iron on top of this pile for about 30 seconds, then move to a different spot until all surfaces of leaves have been covered with wax.

Golden Wheat Wreath

The square shape of this wreath is excellent for framing a mirror or a collage of fall leaves. From your walk in the woods, find four sticks of similar thickness to make the frame. Arrange them with their ends crossed and bind the corners with twine. Cover the sticks with sphagnum moss and wind twine all around to secure the moss to your frame. (Allow the moss to dry before decorating.) Gather golden wheat and allow it to dry. Wire the wheat into little golden bundles, leaving a long enough end of wire to tie the bundles onto your frame. Add a few dried sunflower heads, pine cones, or autumn leaves, attaching them with wire. Finish with a seasonal bow.

Leaf Lightcatcher

Find a particularly large, beautiful autumn leaf. Take two sheets of 8"x10" glass and sandwich the leaf in between. (Glass is available at most framing centers and hardware stores.) Tape all around each edge with 1/2" or 1" wide copper foil tape, leaving a little tape at each end so it can be snipped neatly at a slant in the corner. Burnish the tape down with the tip of a rubber spatula. Prop your leaf in a windowsill to catch the light.

Harvest Moon Buffet

...all the flavors of fall, straight from the garden

Poached Salmon with Dill Sauce
Roast Brisket of Beef
Fresh Tomato Tarts
Roasted Barley Pilaf
Baked Acorn Squash
Roasted Autumn Vegetables
Country Spinach Salad
Honey Poppy Seed Biscuits
Fresh Blueberry Crisp
Brandied Custard Pears

☆ ☆

Ah, pray make no mistake,
We are not shy;
We're very wide awake,
The moon and I!
- Sir William Gilbert

Lentil Soup with Fresh Tomatoes

An easy fall soup, filled with harvest flavors.
Delicious hot or cold.

2 T. olive oil
2 c. onions, peeled and
   chopped
2 cloves garlic, peeled and
   minced
2 bell peppers, red and green,
   seeded and chopped
1 T. fresh thyme, chopped
1/2 c. red wine
1 c. lentils

salt and pepper to taste
2 c. chicken broth
2 c. fresh tomatoes, diced
2 T. fresh rosemary, chopped
1 T. orange zest
1 T. frozen orange juice concentrate, undiluted
fresh chopped basil and
   orange zest for garnish

Heat the olive oil in a large soup pot and sauté the onions, garlic and peppers. Add thyme, wine, lentils, seasonings, and chicken stock to cover. Bring to a boil, then reduce and allow to simmer about 45 minutes, until lentils are tender. Add tomatoes, rosemary, orange zest and orange juice. Garnish with fresh basil and orange zest.

A true harvest moon buffet will include a few rounds and wheels of cheese. Arrange them in a big, shallow basket lined with a pretty remnant of fabric with a fall pattern. Be sure to include an assortment of crackers, breads, fresh grapes and tart red apples.

Poached Salmon with Dill Sauce

Garnish your salmon with thin curls of lemon peel. Serve plenty of lemon alongside!

2 or 3 lb. salmon fillet   court boullion to cover*

Place the salmon fillet in a pot to fit and cover with liquid. Bring to a boil over medium-high heat and then turn off burner. Allow salmon to sit in poaching liquid 25-30 minutes. Remove from water and chill. Transfer to a serving platter and garnish with lemon and dill. Serve with dill sauce.

Court bouillon is made by simmering water with wine or vinegar and vegetables and seasonings such as celery, bay leaves, dill, carrots and coarse salt.

Dill Sauce:

Combine all ingredients and serve with poached or broiled fish.

1 pt. sour cream
1 t. Dijon mustard
1/2 t. salt
2 t. capers (optional)

1/4 t. white pepper
1/2 t. dried or 1 t. fresh dill
    weed, minced
1 T. fresh lemon juice

Cooking is like love. It should be entered into with abandon or not at all.
— Harriet Van Horne

fresh HERBS

Roast Brisket of Beef

So flavorful...tastes even better the second time around!

6 lb. lean brisket of beef
   (first-cut)
2 t. all-purpose flour
black pepper to taste,
   coarsely ground
1 1/2 t. coarse salt

1/4 c. corn oil
8 onions, sliced and
   separated into rings
2 T. tomato paste
2 cloves garlic, chopped

Trim any fat off the brisket and dust with flour. Sprinkle with pepper. Heat the oil in a large Dutch oven and brown the brisket over medium-high heat. Transfer to a dish. Add onion to the Dutch oven and stir, scraping the brown particles and cooking the onions in them until they are soft and brown. Remove from heat and place the brisket and its juices on top of the onions. Spread tomato paste all over the brisket. Sprinkle with salt and pepper and add garlic. (Add a sliced carrot if you wish.) Cover tightly and bake in a preheated 375 degree oven for 90 minutes. Remove the brisket from the oven and transfer to a carving board. Slice it into 1/4-inch thick slices. Return the slices to the Dutch oven, overlapping them in a neat fashion. If pan is very dry, add a bit of water. Cover and return to the oven. Cook another 2 hours, or until meat is fork-tender. Serves 8 as a main course.

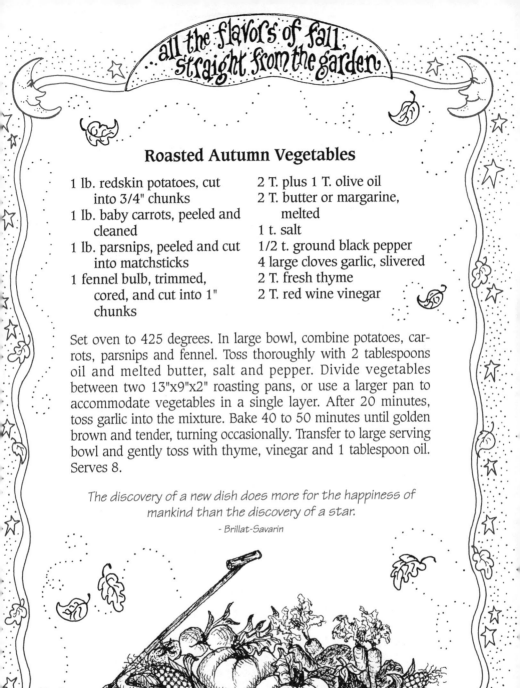

Roasted Autumn Vegetables

1 lb. redskin potatoes, cut
    into 3/4" chunks
1 lb. baby carrots, peeled and
    cleaned
1 lb. parsnips, peeled and cut
    into matchsticks
1 fennel bulb, trimmed,
    cored, and cut into 1"
    chunks

2 T. plus 1 T. olive oil
2 T. butter or margarine,
    melted
1 t. salt
1/2 t. ground black pepper
4 large cloves garlic, slivered
2 T. fresh thyme
2 T. red wine vinegar

Set oven to 425 degrees. In large bowl, combine potatoes, carrots, parsnips and fennel. Toss thoroughly with 2 tablespoons oil and melted butter, salt and pepper. Divide vegetables between two 13"x9"x2" roasting pans, or use a larger pan to accommodate vegetables in a single layer. After 20 minutes, toss garlic into the mixture. Bake 40 to 50 minutes until golden brown and tender, turning occasionally. Transfer to large serving bowl and gently toss with thyme, vinegar and 1 tablespoon oil. Serves 8.

The discovery of a new dish does more for the happiness of mankind than the discovery of a star.
- Brillat-Savarin

Fresh Tomato Tarts

That last, rich bite of summer sunshine.

10 oz. pkg. frozen puff
    pastry shells
2 ripe plum tomatoes
12 t. pesto sauce

Romano cheese, grated
1/8 t. salt
1/8 t. ground black pepper
1/8 t. sugarfresh basil

Thaw pastry shells. Blanch tomatoes in boiling water for a few seconds to loosen skin. Rinse in cold water and remove skin and stem. Slice thinly and drain on paper towel. Roll out pastry shells on floured surface to 5-inch rounds. With tip of knife, cut around edge to make a circle. Make another circle 1/2 inch inside the edge, but do not cut all the way through the dough. Place rounds on ungreased baking sheet. Spread inner circle of each pastry round with 2 teaspoons pesto. Arrange tomato slices on top of pesto; sprinkle with salt, pepper and sugar. Refrigerate 15 minutes. Bake in 375 degree oven 20 to 25 minutes, until puffy and golden brown. Garnish with fresh basil and a sprinkle of grated Romano cheese. Makes 6.

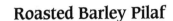

Roasted Barley Pilaf

A hearty, nutty flavor so delicious with beef dishes.

1 T. olive oil
1 c. pearl barley, rinsed
2 shallots, peeled and minced
1/4 lb. mushrooms, sliced

2 c. low-sodium chicken stock
3/4 t. salt
freshly ground pepper

Heat oil over medium heat in heavy saucepan. Add barley and cook 10 minutes, stirring frequently, until it begins to brown. Add shallots and cook another 2 minutes. Add mushrooms and cook 2 minutes, or until wilted. Add stock and salt and bring to a boil; reduce heat and cover. Simmer 45 minutes, or until liquid is absorbed. Stir well and season with pepper before serving.

Baked Acorn Squash

Nature's original soup bowl!

3 medium-sized acorn squash
1 T. brown sugar per half

2 T. butter per half
salt and pepper to taste

Cut squash into halves; remove seeds and fiber. Place cut sides up in ungreased baking pan with 1 inch of water in the bottom. Top each half with butter, maple syrup, salt and pepper. Bake uncovered at 350 degrees about one hour. Serves 6.

Harvest Moon Buffet

Country Spinach Salad

Serve a basket of herbed croutons alongside.

1/2 c. mayonnaise
1/2 c. sour cream
10 oz. spinach, cleaned and
   torn into pieces
1/4 lb. blue cheese, crumbled
2 hard cooked eggs, diced

1 Red Delicious apple,
   unpeeled, cored and diced
1/2 Bermuda onion, sliced
   into thin rings
5 slices bacon, cooked and
   crumbled

Mix mayonnaise and sour cream. Add remaining ingredients and toss well.

Honey Poppy Seed Biscuits

A quick and easy biscuit that's light and tender.

1/2 c. creamed cottage cheese
1/4 c. milk
1 T. poppy seeds

2 T. honey
2 1/4 c. packaged biscuit mix

Combine cottage cheese, milk and honey and blend until almost smooth. Prepare biscuit mix according to package directions, substituting the cheese mixture and poppy seeds for the liquid. Add another 1 or 2 teaspoons milk, if necessary. Bake as directed on package. Makes 12 biscuits.

Fresh Blueberry Crisp

Try raspberries or blackberries, too...whatever's picked fresh that day!

1 1/2 c. flour
1 c. sugar
1 t. ground cinnamon
1 1/2 sticks unsalted butter,
    chilled

10 c. blueberries, rinsed and
    dried
vanilla ice cream

Preheat oven to 375 degrees. Combine flour, sugar and cinnamon. Blend in butter with a pastry cutter or two knives until mixture is crumbly. Place the blueberries in one large or two small buttered baking dishes and generously sprinkle with the crumb mixture. Bake 20-25 minutes. Serve warm with scoops of vanilla ice cream, or top with whipped cream.

The moon was but a chin of gold
A night or two ago,
And now she turns her perfect face
Upon the world below.
—Emily Dickinson

Brandied Custard Pears

Rich custard combined with juicy pears for a delectable fall taste.

4 eggs, beaten
1 1/2 c. light cream
4 T. sugar
2 T. brandy
4 medium-sized, ripe Anjou
    or Bosc pears, sliced

2 T. butter
8-1" thick slices pound
    cake
1/2 c. pecans, toasted and
    broken

In a heavy saucepan, combine eggs, cream and sugar. Cook and stir over medium heat, continuing to cook until it just coats a metal spoon. Remove from heat. Quickly add brandy, and allow to cool by placing the pan in a sink of ice water for about two minutes, stirring constantly. Pour custard into a mixing bowl, cover surface with plastic wrap, and chill till serving time. In a medium skillet, cook the pear slices, covered, in butter over medium-low heat for about 4 minutes; remove cover and cook 2 to 3 minutes longer, or just until tender. Arrange slices of pound cake on each of 8 dessert plates. Spoon pear slices on top of each cake slice. Top each serving with custard, and garnish with toasted pecans.

There are many people who have never tasted a truly ripe pear because they require a bit of patience. After you've purchased them, pears must be allowed to ripen for five to ten days at room temperature. Ripen your pears in a paper bag along with a banana (the banana helps speed the ripening process). Check your pears often by gently pressing down on the stem end with your thumb. When a pear is ripe, it will give slightly. Once it has become soft all over, the inside will be mushy. Pears cannot be eaten right off the tree like apples, as they must be picked while still green to keep from being damaged in shipping. Once you've tasted a truly ripe pear, you're hooked!

Warmhearted things...

Button Napkin Rings

Find lots of colorful toggle buttons in your button box. Then take a length of raffia, narrow paper twist or grosgrain ribbon and thread through the buttons. Arrange four or five buttons per string, combining the colors in a fun way. Tie around rolled cloth napkins, and finish with a bow.

Earring "Charm" Bracelet

Do you wear earrings for pierced ears? The next time you lose a wire-type earring, save the "orphan"! Purchase a gold or sterling wrist chain. Use tweezers or tiny pliers to gently open the connector ring to your earring; then attach to the chain. You can also rescue a dangly pierced earring by stringing it onto a length of cord or chain and wearing it around your neck.

Hallway Hat & Coat Rack

Spiff up your entryway and welcome your friends with a hand-made wall rack...it's easy! Purchase a length of wooden molding. If you would like to paint your wall rack, sand it until it is smooth. Wipe it with clear rubbing alcohol and a soft cloth. Apply a coat of white matte paint with a large paintbrush and allow to dry. Then cover with the color of paint you choose, applying two more coats. When dry, decorate with a "Welcome Friends" message, painted garland of leaves, stencil design or sponge design. Take five or six brass hooks (many styles are available at the hardware store) and secure onto your board at even intervals. Attach your new wall rack with screws or long nails as you would a chair railing, positioning it high enough to accommodate long coats.

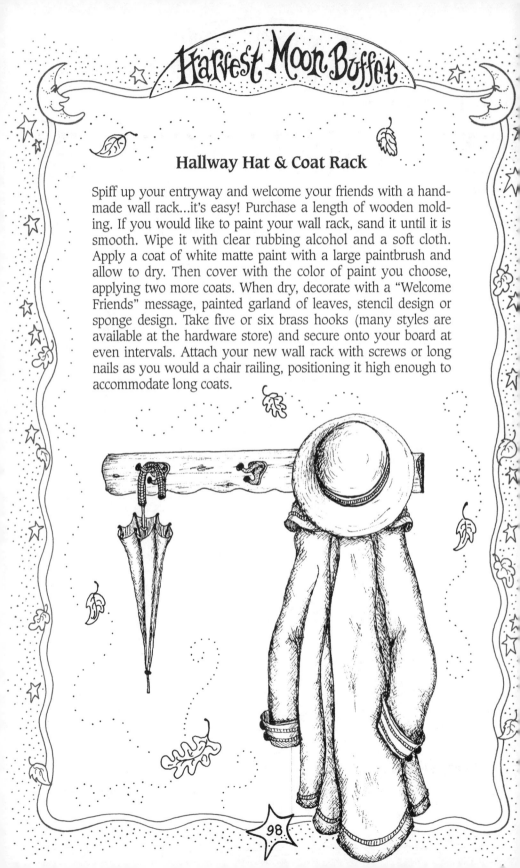

Neighborhood Potluck

...bring a favorite dish, share recipes, make friends

Sensational Snow Peas
Spicy Cheese Tidbits
Prosciutto with Melon on Pumpernickel
Curried Chicken Canapes
Tempting Beer Bread
Date-Pecan Loaf
Baked Ham with Apricot Glaze
Creamy Scalloped Potatoes
Pumpkin Loaf with Caramel Glaze
Rolled Nutmeg Crisps
Chewy Chocolate Cookies
Mulled Cranberry Syllabub

A man hath no better thing under the sun
than to eat, and drink, and to be merry.
- The Bible

Neighborhood Potluck

Sensational Snow Peas

Garnish a big platter of peas with curly strands of orange peel.

100 snow peas

Filling:

2-8 oz. pkg. cream cheese, softened
1/4 c. Parmesan cheese, grated
3 T. catsup
1 1/2 t. dried dill weed

1 t. dry mustard
1 t. Worcestershire sauce
1/2 t. salt
1/2 t. white pepper, freshly ground

Place snow peas in a large bowl and cover with boiling water. Let stand 1 minute. Drain peas and immediately place in ice water. Drain well. Split peas open on seam.

Combine all filling ingredients and mix well. Using pastry tube with 1/4-1/8-inch writing tip, pipe filling into center of each pea pod. Chill until ready to serve. *Note: Filling may be prepared up to 1 week ahead. Stuff peas a day ahead, and refrigerate.*

WELCOME EACH NEW DAY

Spicy Cheese Tidbits

So easy because the bread's already baked. Serve with salsa for dipping.

8 oz. box processed cheese, cubed
1/2 lb. butter, softened
1 t. onion, grated

3-4 dashes of hot pepper sauce
1 egg, beaten
1 loaf whole wheat bread, sliced

Cream together cheese and butter. (Mixture will be lumpy.) Add onion and hot pepper sauce. Add egg. Cut shapes out of bread with cookie cutters. Spread mixture on bread and bake on greased cookie sheet for about 3 minutes at 450 degrees.

Use fun shapes of cookie cutters to cut out bread for canapés...autumn leaves, acorns, crescent moons.

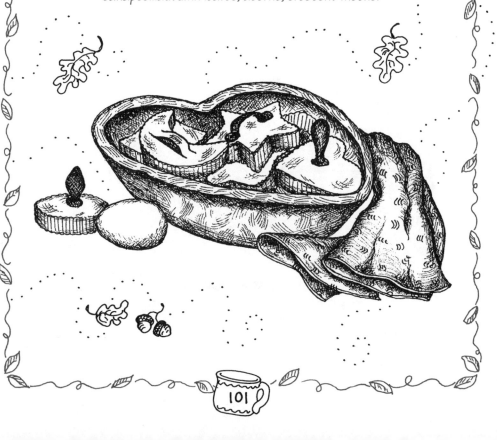

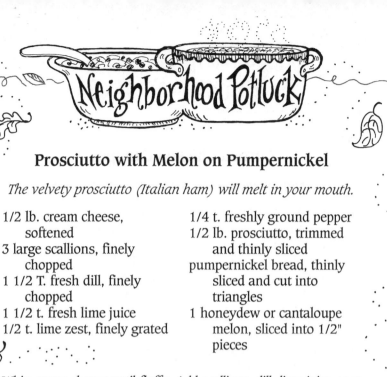

Prosciutto with Melon on Pumpernickel

The velvety prosciutto (Italian ham) will melt in your mouth.

1/2 lb. cream cheese, softened
3 large scallions, finely chopped
1 1/2 T. fresh dill, finely chopped
1 1/2 t. fresh lime juice
1/2 t. lime zest, finely grated

1/4 t. freshly ground pepper
1/2 lb. prosciutto, trimmed and thinly sliced
pumpernickel bread, thinly sliced and cut into triangles
1 honeydew or cantaloupe melon, sliced into 1/2" pieces

Whip cream cheese until fluffy. Add scallions, dill, lime juice, zest and pepper and beat until combined. Arrange prosciutto slices flatly on a large piece of plastic wrap, overlapping them so there are no gaps, to form a large rectangle. Spread the cream cheese mixture evenly over the entire rectangle. Using the plastic wrap as an aid, roll the prosciutto to form a log about 1 1/2" or 2" thick. Wrap in the plastic, seal the ends, and refrigerate overnight. With a sharp knife, slice the log 1/2 or 2 inches thick. Arrange on top of the bread triangles in a platter and garnish with melon slices.

Curried Chicken Canapés

You may try these with sourdough or rye bread, too.

1 c. cooked chicken, minced
1 c. mayonnaise
3/4 c. Monterey Jack cheese, shredded
1/3 c. almonds, ground
1/4 c. fresh parsley, minced
1 t. dried dill weed

2 large shallots, minced
2 t. fresh lemon juice
1 1/2-2 t. curry powder
dash of hot pepper sauce
60 rounds of whole wheat bread, thinly sliced
1/2 lb. slivered almonds

Combine all ingredients except bread and almond slices in large bowl and blend well. Cover and refrigerate until ready to serve. Preheat oven to 500 degrees. Spread 1 1/2 teaspoons of chicken mixture on each round, mounding in center. Top with slivered almonds. Place on baking sheet and bake about 6 minutes, until sizzling. Serve hot.

Tempting Beer Bread

The beer makes the difference.

1/2 c. butter
3 c. self-rising flour

2 T. sugar
12 oz. can of beer

Melt butter and pour 2 tablespoons into a 9"x5" loaf pan to coat. Mix together flour, sugar and beer. Spoon dough into loaf pan. Pour remaining butter over the dough. Bake at 350 for 50-60 minutes, or until bread is golden. Allow to stand 10 minutes; slice with a serrated knife. Serve warm.

Date-Pecan Loaf

Try a slice with a green salad...or have with hot coffee or tea.

1 c. sugar
1/2 c. applesauce
1/2 c. dates, chopped fine
1/3 c. vegetable oil
1 t. baking soda
1/2 t. baking powder

2 eggs
3 t. milk
2 c. flour, sifted
1/4 t. salt
1/4 t. ground nutmeg
3/4 c. pecans, chopped

Topping:

1/4 c. brown sugar, packed
1/4 t. ground cinnamon

1/4 c. pecans, chopped

Combine sugar, applesauce, oil, eggs and milk. Stir in dates. In separate bowl, sift together flour, soda, baking powder, salt and nutmeg. Add to wet mixture and beat until well combined. Stir in pecans. Pour batter into greased loaf pan. Make topping by combining brown sugar, pecans and sprinkle evenly over batter. Bake at 350 degrees for 1 hour. Cover loosely with foil after first 30 minutes of baking. Test with toothpick. Remove from pan and allow to cool.

Baked Ham with Apricot Glaze

A potluck centerpiece with tempting golden-brown glaze.

12 to 14 lb. ready-to-eat ham
    with bone in, skinned
    and trimmed
3 c. apple juice
1 lb. dried apricots

1 c. dark brown sugar
18-20 whole cloves
1/4 c. Dijon mustard
1 c. Madeira wine

With sharp knife, score fatty top of ham in a diamond pattern. Set in a shallow baking pan and spread mustard over top and sides. Insert a clove into each point in the diamond pattern, sprinkle with brown sugar, and pour apple juice into bottom of pan. Bake in preheated 350 degree oven for 1 1/2 hours, basting frequently. While ham is baking, combine apricots and wine in a saucepan and bring to a boil. Cover and remove from heat. After 1 hour of baking time, add apricot mixture to the pan and continue to baste for last half hour.

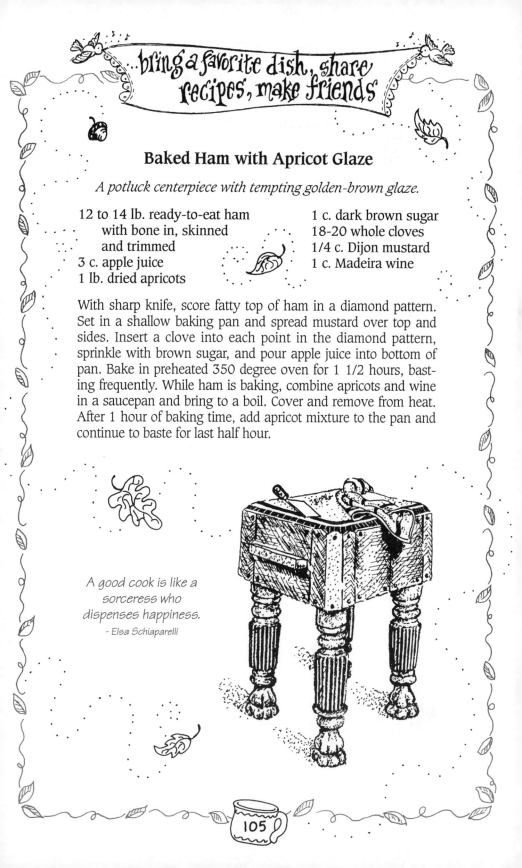

*A good cook is like a
sorceress who
dispenses happiness.*
- Elsa Schiaparelli

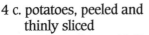

Creamy Scalloped Potatoes

Try making these with red potatoes for a bit of a different texture.

4 c. potatoes, peeled and thinly sliced	1 t. salt
	1/4 t. pepper
2/3 c. Bermuda or Vidalia onion, thinly sliced into rings	2 T. butter
	1 1/2 c. milk, scalded
	1/2 t. paprika
2 T. flour	1/2 c. cheddar cheese, grated

Place layer of potatoes in greased 2-quart casserole and top with 2 tablespoons of onion. Combine flour, salt and pepper, sprinkle over potatoes. Dot with butter. Repeat layers, using remaining potatoes, onion, flour mixture and butter. Pour milk over casserole and sprinkle with paprika. Bake, covered, in 375 degree oven for 45 minutes. Uncover and bake 10 minutes longer; top with cheese. Bake 5 minutes longer, or until cheese is bubbly. Serves 8.

Pumpkin Loaf with Caramel Glaze

If you're short on time, this mix-based pumpkin loaf will be a life-saver!

16 oz. pkg. pumpkin bread mix, prepared according to package directions

Glaze:

2 T. sweet butter	1/3 c. confectioner's sugar
2 T. brown sugar	1/4 t. vanilla
2 T. sugar	pecan halves for garnish
2 T. whipping cream	

In a small saucepan over medium heat, melt butter. Add sugars and whipping cream and bring to a boil. Boil for one minute, stirring constantly. Remove from heat and let cool 20 minutes. Add confectioner's sugar and vanilla; stir until smooth and thick. Spread over cooled pumpkin loaf. Garnish with pecan halves. Serves 12.

Rolled Nutmeg Crisps

Want the perfect cookie for vanilla ice cream? This is it.

3/4 c. butter, softened	2 t. vanilla extract
3/4 c. sugar	1 1/4 c. flour
1/2 t. salt	3 T. confectioner's sugar
1/4 t. nutmeg, freshly grated	nutmeg, freshly grated, as
3 egg whites	topping

Blend together butter, sugar, salt and nutmeg until just mixed. Gradually add egg whites and vanilla; beat well. Add flour and mix well. Cover and chill dough 1 hour. Drop by teaspoonfuls 2 inches apart onto greased cookie sheet. Bake in preheated 375 degree oven 6 to 8 minutes, or until edges are lightly browned. Remove cookies from oven and, working quickly, carefully roll each cookie into a thin tube-shape. Place on cooling rack seam side down. Cookies will become crisp as they cool. Sprinkle with confectioner's sugar and freshly grated nutmeg. Makes 3 dozen.

Old friendships are the dearest.

Chewy Chocolate Cookies

Make enough for friends to take home. Wrap in cellophane and tie with a ribbon.

1 1/4 c. butter, softened
2 c. sugar
2 eggs
2 t. vanilla

2 c. flour
3/4 c. unsweetened cocoa
1 t. baking soda
1/2 t. salt

Cream butter and sugar. Add eggs and vanilla and mix well. Combine flour, cocoa, baking soda and salt; blend into creamed mixture. Drop by teaspoonfuls onto ungreased cookie sheets. Bake 8-9 minutes at 350 degrees; do not overbake. Cookies will be soft. They will puff during baking and flatten during cooling. Makes 4 1/2 dozen.

Mulled Cranberry Syllabub

Float a colorful orange slice in each mug.

1 qt. cranberry juice cocktail
18 oz. can pineapple juice
3 cinnamon sticks
1 t. whole allspice
1 t. whole cloves

dash ground nutmeg
1/2 t. orange extract
1/2 t. lemon extract
cinnamon sticks for garnish

Combine first 6 ingredients in large saucepan. Bring mixture to a boil; reduce heat and simmer, covered, 20 minutes. Remove from heat; strain. Stir in extracts. Serve hot with sticks of cinnamon. Serves 8.

Spicy creations...

Cinnamon-Orange Potpourri

4 oz. cinnamon pieces, 1/4"
   or smaller
3 oz. whole allspice
2 oz. orange peel, minced
1 oz. whole cloves
1 oz. rosemary leaves

1 oz. oakmoss, cut and sifted
1/2 oz. nutmeg, crushed
1/2 oz. ginger, cut and sifted
14 drops ea. of cinnamon,
   allspice, and sweet
   orange oil

Combine all spices and oils and allow to set, covered, for at least three weeks. Use this potpourri mixture in bowls and baskets all around the house, or tie up in little fabric pouches and give it as gifts to your friends. This recipe makes about a pound.

Did you know that cloves are really flower buds, and that cinnamon is from the bark of a tree? Allspice is a berry, and nutmeg is a fruit pit.

Apple Cones

Take a very large pine cone and level it by rocking it gently back and forth on a solid surface. Take small slices of dried apples, fold, and insert them snugly between the cone petals, skin side out. (Use hot glue to secure the slices to the cone.) Insert small sprigs of baby's breath all around the cone. Tie narrow satin ribbons into tiny bows and glue them on the edges of the cone's petals. Sprinkle a few drops of essential oil on the edges of your cone. Hang in a doorway, bedroom or bath, or give as a gift.

Spice Necklace

Select whole spices, such as cloves, vanilla, cardamom, cinnamon sticks, nutmegs and star anise. Soak the spices in water for a day, then strain and let them dry on an old towel. Cut the very large pieces with a sharp scissors. You can then drill tiny holes into the spices, or force a large sewing needle through them to string a necklace. Use a heavy-duty carpet thread that can take the strain. A large, perfect star anise makes a beautiful center "bead" for your necklace. You may want to add little wooden beads to your design, for added color.

Remembering Thanksgiving

...a bounty of savory traditional fare

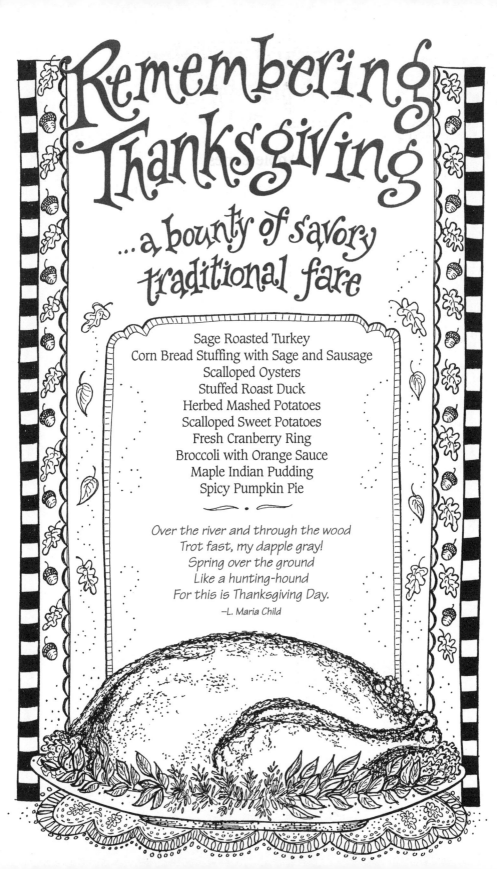

Sage Roasted Turkey
Corn Bread Stuffing with Sage and Sausage
Scalloped Oysters
Stuffed Roast Duck
Herbed Mashed Potatoes
Scalloped Sweet Potatoes
Fresh Cranberry Ring
Broccoli with Orange Sauce
Maple Indian Pudding
Spicy Pumpkin Pie

Over the river and through the wood
Trot fast, my dapple gray!
Spring over the ground
Like a hunting-hound
For this is Thanksgiving Day.
—L. Maria Child

Sage Roasted Turkey

12-14 lb. turkey
1 bunch fresh sage leaves
1/2 t. salt
1/2 t. black pepper, freshly ground
1/2 c. butter, melted

Remove giblets and neck from turkey, set aside. Rinse turkey under running water; drain well and pat dry thoroughly with paper towels. Sprinkle inside and out with salt and pepper. Gently loosen skin flesh. Arrange as many sage leaves as desired under the skin. Pat skin back into place. Loosely stuff neck and body cavities with stuffing. Close both cavities with skewers. Tie legs together; tuck wings under body. Place turkey, breast side up, on rack in shallow roasting pan. Brush all over with melted butter. Roast 15 minutes at 425 degrees. Reduce temperature to 325 degrees and roast 4 to 4 1/2 hours or longer, continuing to baste with drippings, until breast skin is crisp and golden and juices run clear when thigh is pricked with fork. (If turkey is browning too quickly, it may be covered loosely with foil. Meat thermometer should register 180 degrees.) Serves 12 to 14.

Cornbread Stuffing with Sage and Sausage

1 day-old, 8" square
  cornbread
1 lb. sweet Italian sausage,
  browned, drained and
  crumbled
2 small onions, finely
  chopped
1 c. chicken stock

salt and pepper to taste
2 cloves garlic, peeled and
  minced
1/2 c. pine nuts, toasted
  (optional)
6 ribs celery, finely chopped
1 T. dried sage
4 T. unsalted butter, melted

Cut cornbread into 1/2" cubes and spread evenly on a baking sheet. Toast in 350 degree oven about 20 minutes, or until golden. Heat a large skillet over medium-high heat and brown sausage 6 to 8 minutes, until brown. Drain into a bowl, reserving 1 teaspoon of fat in the pan. Add onions to skillet and cook until translucent. Add celery and garlic and cook until celery is soft. Combine sausage, the onion mixture, cornbread, pine nuts and sage in a large bowl and mix well. Add chicken stock and melted butter and toss to combine. Season with salt and pepper to taste. Allow to cool before stuffing turkey. Makes 10 cups, enough to stuff a 14 pound turkey with some left over for a separate baking dish.

Baked squash is delicious stuffed with sausage dressing or raisins and chopped apples. Try a little cooked, crumbled bacon on top. Yum!

Scalloped Oysters

3 pints oysters, drained, with
    juice reserved
2 c. coarse cracker crumbs

1/2 c. butter, melted
salt and pepper to taste
3/4 c. milk

Check each oyster for shells and remove. Put one layer of cracker crumbs and one layer of oysters in a well-buttered casserole. Sprinkle with salt and pepper and drizzle butter over the top. Continue to layer oysters, crumbs, seasonings and butter, ending with cracker crumbs. Mix oyster juice and milk. Pour over top of casserole. Drizzle with remaining butter. Bake uncovered at 375 degrees for 30-40 minutes.

Thanksgiving originated as three days of prayer and feasting celebrated by the Plymouth colonists in 1621. President George Washington proclaimed the first national Thanksgiving Day on November 26, 1789. In 1863, President Abraham Lincoln declared Thanksgiving an annual holiday to be celebrated on the last Thursday in November. The Thanksgiving menu hasn't changed much from the original one of roast turkey, stuffing, cranberry sauce, and pumpkin pie. These are the main dishes of the New England harvest home feast, and have remained favorites to this day.

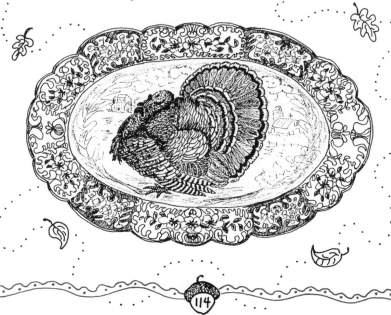

Stuffed Roast Duck

This is a little different way to prepare duck. It is very moist and flavorful!

4 lb. duck
salt and pepper to taste

1 qt. sauerkraut

Remove and discard the gizzard, liver, heart and neck. Rinse thoroughly inside and out. Dry well on paper towels. Season inside with salt and pepper. Stuff cavity and neck loosely with sauerkraut. Place on rack in a shallow pan. Prick the skin several times. Bake at 325 degrees for 2 1/2 hours. For a colorful garnish, add vegetables such as carrots, onions and Brussels sprouts to roasting pan during last 40 minutes of cooking.

The maple wears a gayer scarf,
The field a scarlet gown.
Lest I should be old-fashioned,
I'll put a trinket on.
—Emily Dickinson

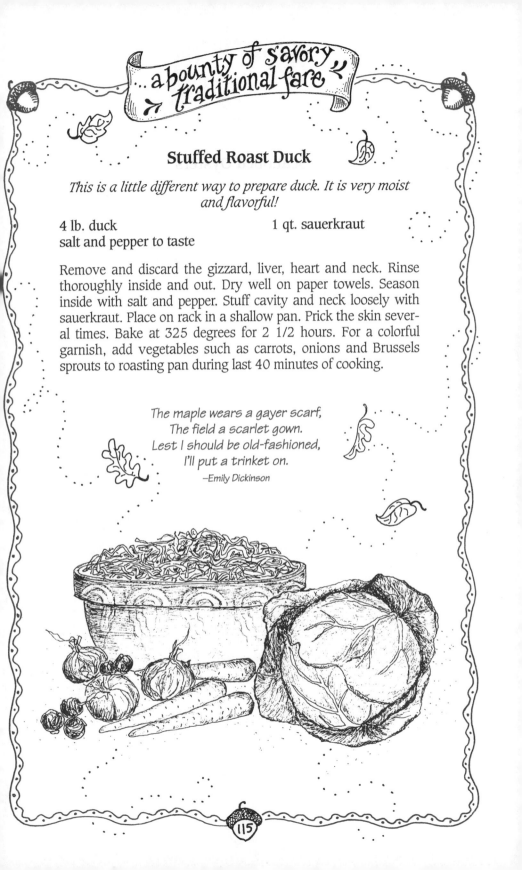

Herbed Mashed Potatoes

These can be made with either sour cream or cream cheese.
Delicious!

6 1/2 c. baking potatoes,
   peeled and cubed
2 garlic cloves, halved
1/2 c. milk
1/2 c. sour cream
2 T. fresh parsley, minced

2 T. fresh oregano, minced
1 T. fresh thyme, minced
1 T. butter
3/4 t. salt
1/8 t. pepper

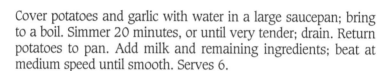

Cover potatoes and garlic with water in a large saucepan; bring to a boil. Simmer 20 minutes, or until very tender; drain. Return potatoes to pan. Add milk and remaining ingredients; beat at medium speed until smooth. Serves 6.

Scalloped Sweet Potatoes

Hearty, healthy, and a family favorite.

4 lbs. sweet potatoes, peeled
   and sliced lengthwise
3 1/2 c. milk
1/4 c. butter

salt and pepper to taste
1 c. light brown sugar, firmly
   packed

In heavy saucepan, combine sweet potatoes with milk and bring to a boil over moderate heat. Add salt and pepper. Transfer mixture to a greased 14" gratin dish and bake, covered in a 400 degree oven for 20 minutes. Reduce the heat to 350 degrees and bake, covered, 20 minutes more. Sprinkle potatoes with brown sugar and dot with butter. Bake, uncovered, 10 minutes longer. Serves 8.

Hurrah for the fun!
Is the turkey done?
Hurrah for the pumpkin pie!
—Lydia Maria Child

Fresh Cranberry Ring

Beautiful served on a cut glass plate with cool, green grapes.

2 c. fresh, raw cranberries, chopped in food processor
1/2 t. lemon rind, grated
3/4 c. sugar
1/2 c. cold water

2 envelopes unflavored gelatin
1 c. red wine, heated
1/2 c. walnuts, chopped
2 T. fresh lemon juice
1/2 c. mayonnaise

Chop cranberries in a blender or food processor, stir in lemon rind and sugar, and set aside in a bowl. Pour cold water in the blender and sprinkle gelatin on the water. Allow to soften 10 minutes. Heat the wine to almost boiling and add to the blender. Blend until gelatin has dissolved. Mix cranberries, walnuts, lemon juice and mayonnaise with the gelatin mixture and pour into a wet 1 1/2-quart ring mold. Refrigerate until set.

Frosted fruit garnishes are easy. Just coat grapes or berries with egg white and dip in super-fine sugar. You can process regular sugar in your food processor to make it extra fine. Arrange fruits on a pretty, cut-glass plate around a festive spice cake. The flavor of fresh fruit is delicious when combined with a rich, spicy dessert. Serve whipped cream on the side.

Broccoli with Orange Sauce

1 lb. fresh broccoli, cut into
   spears
2 T. butter
1 T. cornstarch
1 c. fresh orange juice
1 T. fresh parsley, minced

1 T. lemon juice
1 T. orange peel, grated
1/2 t. dried thyme
1/2 t. dry mustard
1/4 t. pepper

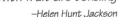

Steam broccoli just until tender. In separate saucepan, melt butter. Blend in cornstarch and 1/2 cup orange juice, stirring until blended. Mix in remaining orange juice, parsley, lemon juice, orange peel, thyme, mustard, and pepper. Cook over moderate heat until mixture thickens. Pour over broccoli. Garnish with thin slices of orange, or bright slivers of orange peel.

> *The golden-rod is yellow.*
> *The corn is turning brown:*
> *The trees in apple orchards*
> *With fruit are bending down.*
> —Helen Hunt Jackson

Maple Indian Pudding

1 c. cornmeal
1 qt. whole milk
1/2 c. light brown sugar

1 c. heavy cream
1/2 c. pure maple syrup
1/8 t. freshly grated nutmeg

Butter a 1 1/2-quart soufflé dish. In heavy saucepan, whisk cornmeal into the milk over moderately high heat, stirring until slightly thickened, about 5 minutes. Remove from heat and stir in the brown sugar. Add cream, maple syrup and nutmeg. Pour in the prepared dish and bake in a 275 degree oven about 4 hours, until pudding is bubbly and top is brown. Allow to rest 30 minutes before serving.

For pottage and puddings and custards and pies
Our pumpkins and parsnips are common supplies;
We have pumpkin at morning and pumpkin at noon,
If it was not for pumpkin, we should be undone.

- American Folk song

Spicy Pumpkin Pie

Double-Crust Pastry:

2 1/4 c. all-purpose flour
1/2 t. salt
1 stick cold unsalted butter,
    cut into 1/2" pieces

3 T. cold vegetable shortening
4 to 5 T. ice water

Combine the flour and salt in a food processor and pulse a few times to mix. Add the butter and shortening and process until the mixture is textured with particles the size of peas. Add 3 tablespoons of the ice water, 1 tablespoon at a time, pulsing briefly after each addition. Add another tablespoon of water and pulse until the dough begins to hold together. Add the last table-spoon of water only if necessary. Place the dough on a lightly floured surface and gather into a ball, handling it as little as pos-sible. Divide the dough in half to make two crusts. Pat the dough into disks, wrap in wax paper and refrigerate for at least 30 minutes before rolling out. Enough for 2-9-inch pie shells.

Pumpkin Pie:

29 oz. can of solid-pack
    pumpkin
2 c. light brown sugar, firmly
    packed
3 T. pumpkin pie spice

1 t. salt
5 large eggs, lightly beaten
2-12 oz. cans evaporated milk
fresh whipped cream for
    garnish

In a large bowl, whisk pumpkin, brown sugar, spice and salt. Whisk in the eggs. Slowly whisk in the milk until completely blended. Refrigerate. Roll the prepared pastry into 11-inch rounds and fit into 9-inch pie pans. Fit the dough against the bottom and sides without stretching. Trim the excess dough to about 1/2-inch. Fold it under and crimp or press into a pattern. Prick the dough all over with a fork. Freeze the sheets for 30 minutes. In a preheated, 375 degree oven, bake the shells for 10 minutes, or until they begin to brown slightly. Allow to cool to room temperature. Pour the filling into the cooled pie shells and bake for about 45 minutes, until the pies move very slight-ly in one mass when lightly jiggled. Transfer to a rack for cool-ing. Serve with plenty of freshly whipped cream.

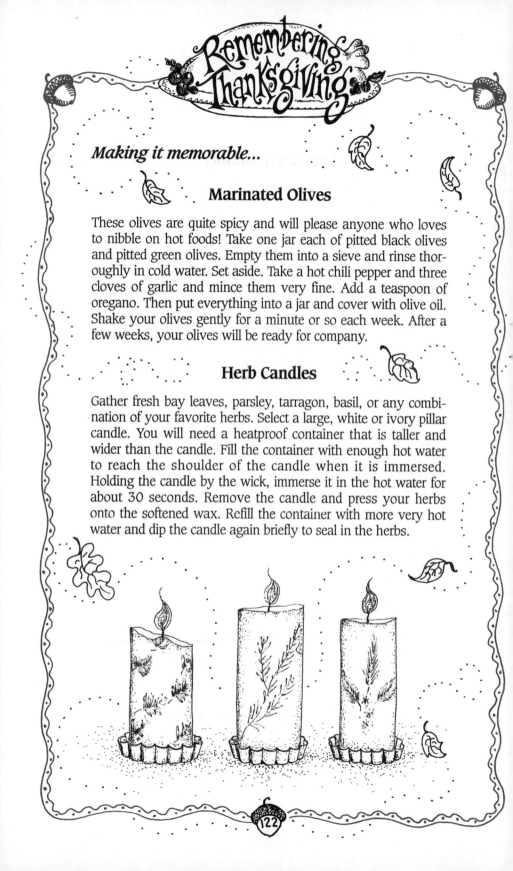

Making it memorable...

Marinated Olives

These olives are quite spicy and will please anyone who loves to nibble on hot foods! Take one jar each of pitted black olives and pitted green olives. Empty them into a sieve and rinse thoroughly in cold water. Set aside. Take a hot chili pepper and three cloves of garlic and mince them very fine. Add a teaspoon of oregano. Then put everything into a jar and cover with olive oil. Shake your olives gently for a minute or so each week. After a few weeks, your olives will be ready for company.

Herb Candles

Gather fresh bay leaves, parsley, tarragon, basil, or any combination of your favorite herbs. Select a large, white or ivory pillar candle. You will need a heatproof container that is taller and wider than the candle. Fill the container with enough hot water to reach the shoulder of the candle when it is immersed. Holding the candle by the wick, immerse it in the hot water for about 30 seconds. Remove the candle and press your herbs onto the softened wax. Refill the container with more very hot water and dip the candle again briefly to seal in the herbs.

Cherries in Brandy

Only use the very best canned cherries you can find for this hostess gift. Drain syrup from a can of cherries into a saucepan, add a cinnamon stick and 3 tablespoons of sugar. Stir constantly while bringing to a boil. Allow to cool and strain into a jar. Fill another jar with the cherries, sorting out any that are imperfect. Fill the jar with 1/4 cup brandy. Tighten the lid and store in a cool place for 3 or 4 weeks. Repack the cherries in a fancy glass jar, adding a cinnamon stick. Decorate with a bow tied to a cinnamon stick. These cherries are delicious over a mound of vanilla ice cream!

Bouquet Garnis

A traditional bouquet garnis is made from three or four sprigs of parsley, two sprigs of thyme and a bay leaf tied together with a string. You can make a nice little bunch of bouquet garnis using the same herbs, only chopped fine. Cut out circles of gauze or cheesecloth and place 2 heaping teaspoons of herbs in each circle. Gather the cloth circles around the herbs and tie in little bundles with clean white string so they can be added to a soup or stew, infusing it with wonderful flavor. Put several of these bundles into a pretty glass jar and tie with a ribbon...makes a thoughtful hostess gift!

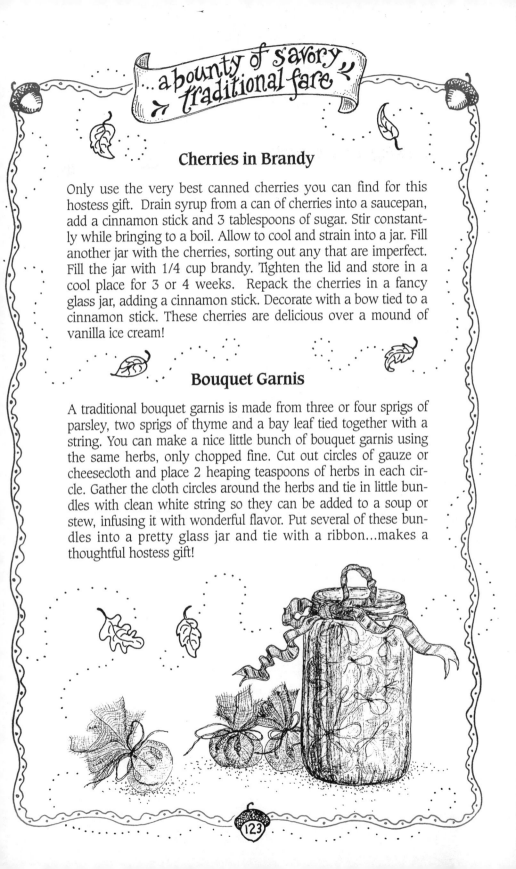

Index

Gooseberry Patch Originals

HOMESPUN CHRISTMAS
A heartwarming collection of Christmas recipes, tips and ideas

BUMBLEBEES & BUTTERFLIES
A garden Journal with plenty of space for all your garden-fresh recipes

SLEIGHBELLS & MISTLETOE
A Christmas Journal for jotting down all your best holiday ideas

TEACUPS & GINGERBREAD
A kitchen Journal for recording your favorite recipes & ideas

Gooseberry Patch Originals

WELCOME HOME for the HOLIDAYS

your companion from September through December

from harvest through Christmas... a treasury of holiday recipes, decorating tips, traditions & easy-to-make gifts

OLD-FASHIONED COUNTRY CHRISTMAS

A holiday keepsake of recipes, traditions, homemade gifts, decorating ideas, & favorite childhood memories

OLD-FASHIONED COUNTRY COOKIES hundreds of recipes, tips, & ideas

Yummy recipes, tips, traditions, how-to's, and sweet memories... everything Cookies!

OLD-FASHIONED COUNTRY CHRISTMAS our all-time BEST SELLER!

GOOD FOR YOU! recipes, fun ideas, heartwarming stories, good for body, mind, soul

FOR BEES & ME garden-fresh recipes, backyard entertaining & gifts from the garden

A Bouquet of garden-fresh Recipes, Simple Pleasures, Memories, Hints, Backyard Entertainment & Easy-To-Make Gifts, Herbal Beauty Potions

Good For You!

A collection of good food, good fun, & good stories for the body, mind & soul!

GOOSEBERRY PATCH
P.O. Box 190, Dept. CELA
Delaware, OH 43015

Please send me the following Gooseberry Patch books:

Book	Quantity	Price	Total
Old-Fashioned Country Christmas	————	$14.95	————
Welcome Home for the Holidays	————	$14.95	————
Old-Fashioned Country Cookies	————	$14.95	————
For Bees & Me	————	$17.95	————
Good For You!	————	$14.95	————
Homespun Christmas	————	$14.95	————
Celebrate Autumn	————	$12.95	————
Celebrate Winter	————	$12.95	————
		Merchandise Total	————
		Ohio Residents add 5 1/2%	————

Shipping & handling: Add $2 for each book. Call for special delivery prices.

Total ————

Quantity discounts and special shipping prices available when purchasing 6 or more books. Call and ask! Wholesale inquiries invited.

Name: _____

Address: _____

City: _____ State: _____ Zip: _____

GOOSEBERRY PATCH
P.O. Box 190, Dept. CELA
Delaware, OH 43015

♡ How to Order ♡
For faster service on credit card orders,
call toll-free 1·800·85·GOOSE!
(1·800·854·6673)

Please send me the following Gooseberry Patch books:

Book	Quantity	Price	Total
Old-Fashioned Country Christmas	————	$14.95	————
Welcome Home for the Holidays	————	$14.95	————
Old-Fashioned Country Cookies	————	$14.95	————
For Bees & Me	————	$17.95	————
Good For You!	————	$14.95	————
Homespun Christmas	————	$14.95	————
Celebrate Autumn	————	$12.95	————
Celebrate Winter	————	$12.95	————
		Merchandise Total	————
		Ohio Residents add 5 1/2%	————

Shipping & handling: Add $2 for each book. Call for special delivery prices.

Total ————

Quantity discounts and special shipping prices available when purchasing 6 or more books. Call and ask! Wholesale inquiries invited.

Name: _____

Address: _____

City: _____ State: _____ Zip: _____

We accept checks, money orders, Visa or MasterCard (please include expiration date). Payable in U.S. funds only. Prices subject to change.

squash first day of school turkey & d

stuffed apple·picking frosty fields * * piles of leaves veggies

fresh s'mores flying footballs glowing campfires